# Portuguese for Beginners

*Learn Portuguese in 30 Days the Easy Way*

# Table of Contents

# Introduction

The title says it all – and if you are reading this, you are obviously pondering on giving Portuguese a go. So, the question just has to be: why buy this book out of the endless options in the market? What makes this one the right book for you? The truth is that, unlike other books that claim to teach you Portuguese, this book is not a manual that you read once or twice in hopes of mastering a couple of greetings and memorizing short dialogues to get through interactions when in a Portuguese-speaking country.

Portuguese for Beginners – Learn Portuguese in 30 Days Without Wasting Any Time – aims to, firstly, give you a solid foundation of the Portuguese language, its history, and the basics – from which it then builds on to arm you with the proverbial knowledge of fishing, instead of the fish – it is a tool rather than a solution.

To do that, without it being a complex manual for the already advanced speaker, Portuguese for Beginners – Learn Portuguese in 30 Days Without Wasting Any Time –  adopts a very hands-on method, namely the Harmer's teaching method, or the **PPP** approach – present, practice, produce –  in which you start by being introduced to the subject at hand, then practice what was taught, having subsequently to produce the material on your own, before moving on to the next chapter.[1]

In the presentation stage of this book, there is an attempt to raise interest in the chosen topic in a contextualized way, but to prevent the lesson from becoming too boring, the *practice stage* dedicates itself to the structure and important rules that have to be followed so that the material is learned correctly. The third and final phase – the production phase – focuses on fluency. In this stage, you will be given the opportunity to *produce* a personalized version of what was just learned. This stage is pivotal for knowledge retention as it tests your understanding of the chapter and full comprehension of the material, not just your memory skills.

Though very challenging, this approach is great for beginners, even though it requires hard work and repetition. A book that promises to teach you an idiom while claiming the feat to be easy would be misleading – amd probably not teaching you properly.

Thus, you can expect an enticing yet demanding journey, great for beginners and intermediate learners alike, that sets out to teach Portuguese from its roots, moving on to its pillars, so you can put a solid roof over the rich house that the Portuguese language is – all within a month.

So now, just sit back and buckle up – it's going to be an exciting ride!

---

[1] If you want to know more about this teaching method, you can start out by checking the following paper by Criado, Raquel. "A critical review of the presentation-practice-production model (PPP) in foreign language teaching." *Homenaje a francisco gutiérrez díez* (2013): 97-115, available for free at https://d1wqtxts1xzle7.cloudfront.net/31583876/Criado_A_critical_Review_of_PPP_2013-with-cover-page-v2.pdf?Expires=1665166226&Signature=dJCYYOQUpHdj1U1CW7QP7BstPFESmWD Tnxe92glQ4L3qvVdX0nTTiY2YrhCmcsaG5XfN23H297QdCUI6Qzn~UeSO~cg6egV2 5GvoJfgrbA9vQa5v343FMQ9tL3gQf6921lmHg2qdx1PeVRFl578FeX5~MIjy8q2NrCrlcI LucUW6ahOzGT0xScLD47rn2ctnzBTzaXg9JscDZH84yL4iCl8zq2AAke8AsxWC8~v-PsA-giw33iqp87rOdguy3WSQjWqdbScG5U02c2lAZClyiWG3Xz~1anRzZiY~MZ3smfIQrN AExngijCKOWpQBMB3XwHc7ovQaO993d2zHSn2G9kA__&Key-Pair-Id=APKAJLOHF5GGSLRBV4ZA

# Chapter 1: Portuguese Basics

«*Seated and seatbelt fastened, I'm finally on the plane to Lisbon for my 30-days holiday! But hey: I don't know how to speak Portuguese! How will I get around? Well, I better get to it then, right here and right now. Luckily, I can start by checking out the Portuguese pamphlet this airline conveniently provides – it should help me with the first stages of this exciting quest!*»

## 1.1 Brief history of the Portuguese language

As the official language of Portugal, Brazil, Cape Verde, Guinea-Bissau, Equatorial Guinea, São Tomé and Príncipe, East Timor, and Macau, aside from being spoken by a significant minority in several other countries like France, Uruguay, Luxembourg, and Switzerland – just to name a few – Portuguese is the sixth most-spoken language in the whole planet, with over 255 million speakers worldwide.

Its history is both rich and long, with its first form dating back to the XI century. Since it is a few centuries old, perhaps it is no surprise that Portuguese is a Romance language that actually has its roots in vulgar Latin since this was the idiom spoken by the Romans that were occupying what is now the Portuguese territory, thus sharing many traits to other Romance languages like French, Spanish or Catalan. It also has been influenced by other tribes that were established or invaded the Iberian Peninsula throughout history, such as the Celts, Moors, and Visigoths.

Evidently, back then, the language was very different from how it is spoken and written in the current times. That evolution and development are still seen nowadays, with attempts to standardize and unify the nuances of the different types of Portuguese that are spoken throughout the world. More recently, for instance, the Orthographic Agreement of 1990, which only came into effect in Portugal in 2010, has changed the spelling of many words so that the writing matches the spoken language more seamlessly. As a result, on occasion, you may still see different spellings of the same word since the adaptation has not been fully integrated yet by all speakers.[2]

Alright, now let us move on from the history and get back to the present!

## 1.2 The Alphabet and Accents

Learning the Portuguese alphabet may very well be the easiest thing you'll do today: its alphabet is just like the English one – it consists of 26 letters, as it is based on the Latin alphabet, as you now well know. So, we have the vowels: A, E, I, O, and U, and the consonants: B, C, D, F, G, H, J, K, L, M, N, P, Q, R, S, T, V, X, W, Y, and Z.

In spite of sharing its letters with the English language, the Portuguese pronunciation of its alphabet might prove a little bit more difficult since it differs in many cases. Actually, many sounds that exist in the Portuguese language *don't exist* in the English language! Furthermore, accents or diacritical marks change the sound of letters.

So, when it comes to vowels, there are four types of diacritical marks that may be used:

---

[2] The new agreement is still a source of controversy among several native speakers, so many choose to not follow it.

| | |
|---|---|
| Acute accent | ´ |
| Circumflex mark | ^ |
| Grave stress | ` |
| Tilde | ~ |

These accent marks change not only the sound of the vowel but also indicate the syllable that should be stressed.

When it comes to consonants, there is only one letter that may have a diacritic – the "c," with a cedilla under it:

| | |
|---|---|
| Cedilla | ç |

No worries, though, as there will be plenty of examples and tips to help with the pronunciation of the words.

# 1.3 Pronunciation

As for the vowels, there can be four types of pronunciation – a) open, b) closed, c) reduced, and d) nasal.

## a) Open pronunciation

It is, more often than not, the correct way of pronouncing the vowels whenever they are in the stressed syllable. The trick is to open your lips when pronouncing the vowel.

- When it comes to the letter "A," it should sound like the "A" in "BAR";
- When it comes to the letter "E," it should sound like the "E" in "SET";
- When it comes to the letter "I," it should sound like the "EE" in "FEET";
- When it comes to the letter "O," it should sound like the "O" in "SHOT";

- When it comes to the letter "U," it should sound like the "U" in "NUDE."

## b) Closed pronunciation

The trick to closed pronunciation, on the other hand, is to close the lips while saying the vowels.

- When it comes to the letter "A," it should sound like the "U" in "HUM." It's the usual sound it makes when an "A" is at the end of a word;
- When it comes to the letter "E," it should sound like the "E" in "POSE";
- When it comes to the letter "I," there really isn't a closed pronunciation;
- When it comes to the letter "O," it should sound like the "O" in "SOAP";
- When it comes to the letter "U," there really isn't a closed pronunciation either.

## c) Reduced pronunciation

The reduced pronunciation occurs mainly when the vowel is at the end of a word. A tip for pronouncing it better is to try and stop yourself short before finishing the word.

- When it comes to the letter "A," there really isn't a reduced pronunciation;
- When it comes to the letter "E," it sounds very similar to the closed pronunciation;
- When it comes to the letter "I," there really isn't a reduced pronunciation;
- When it comes to the letter "O," it should sound like the "O" in "LOSE";
- When it comes to the letter "U," there really isn't a reduced pronunciation either.

## d) Nasal pronunciation

The nasal pronunciation is, simply put, how you would talk if you were sick and had your nose all clogged up. You can practice by covering your nostrils with your hands to say the words that should have nasal sounds. It usually occurs whenever the vowel precedes an "M" or an "N."

- When it comes to the letter "A," it should sound like the "UN" in "SUNG";
- When it comes to the letter "E," it should sound like the "EM" in "EMPATHY";
- When it comes to the letter "I," it should sound like the "IN" in "SINGLE";
- When it comes to the letter "O," it should sound like the "ON" in "LONG";
- When it comes to the letter "U," it should sound like the "OUND" in "WOUND."

Regarding consonants, the pronunciation is very similar to how the letters sound in English; however, there may be slight differences not depending on diacritical marks but on the location of the consonant – whether it is between vowels or if it is at the start of a word, for instance.

The following table displays the letters that are pronounced in several different ways in Portuguese. The omitted letters are pronounced just like they are in English.

| C | before an "E" or "I" | <u>C</u>ELLAR |
| C | before "A," "O," "U," or any consonant | <u>C</u>ALL |
| C | before an "H" | <u>SH</u>ORT[3] |

---

3 Note that the "CH" sound in Portuguese is similar but not exactly equal to the "CH" in English. The "SH" pair in English, however, sounds exactly like the "CH" should.

| | | |
|---|---|---|
| G | before "A," "O," "U" | **G**OLD |
| G | before an "E" or "I" | SEI**Z**URE[4] |
| H | always silent | **(H)**AM[5] |
| J | before any vowel | SEI**Z**URE |
| L | beginning of a word | **L**OST |
| L | middle or end of a word | PA**L**E |
| L | before an "H" | *no equivalent*[6] |
| M | beginning of a word and between vowels | **M**ORE |
| M | end of a word | FO**N**T[7] |

---

4 The soft "G" in a word like "gel," for instance, doesn't quite capture the right sound. In English, it's almost like there is a "D" before the "G" in cases like those. Another example of what the pronunciation should sound like is the letter "S" in the word "measure."

5 Just like any word would sound if there wasn't an "H" to begin with.

6 Jump to chapter with the IPA Chart to know more about this diphthong.

7 The "M" at the end of a word in Portuguese doesn't quite sound like it does at the end of an English word. Like the example given, it's closer to the nasal sound of an "N" between a vowel and consonant, than to the pronunciation of the "M" in "album," for instance.

| | | |
|---|---|---|
| N | beginning of a word and between vowels | HO<u>N</u>OR |
| N | between vowel and consonant | CA<u>N</u>'T |
| N | before an "H" | *no equivalent*[8] |
| Q(u) | before an "E" or "I" | <u>KI</u>LOMETRE |
| Q(u) | before "A," "O," "U" | <u>QUA</u>LM |
| R | end of a word, or before or after a vowel | BA<u>R</u> |
| R | beginning of a word or next to another "R" | *no equivalent*[9] |
| S | beginning of a word or next to another "S" | <u>S</u>OAP |
| S | before a consonant | <u>SH</u>OE |

---

8 Jump to chapter with the **IPA Chart** to know more about this diphthong.

9 Jump to chapter with the **IPA Chart** to know more about this particular sound.

| | | |
|---|---|---|
| S | between two vowels | <u>Z</u>OMBIE |
| X[10] | usually after two vowels or after "EN" | <u>SH</u>OE |
| X | *no rule* | BO<u>X</u> |
| X | usually between vowels | <u>Z</u>OMBIE |
| X | *no rule* | <u>S</u>OAP |
| Z | end of a word | <u>SH</u>OE |
| Z | any other position | <u>Z</u>OMBIE |

As stated before, diacritical marks can also change the sound of a vowel. So, when it comes to the acute accent, it's quite straightforward – the vowel in question adopts an open sound.

The circumflex mark, on the other hand, makes the vowels adopt the closed pronunciation. It is only used above the vowels "a," "e," and "o."

A tilde over a vowel should make it sound nasal. It is only used above the vowels "a" and "o."

The grave accent, however, doesn't actually indicate a different pronunciation from the ones we have already seen; rather, its purpose is to indicate the contraction of words. The most common example is the contraction between the definite article "a (the)" and the preposition "a (to)." So, in the sentence "I went to the school –

---

10 Even though these are the typical cases, there are many exceptions to the rule regarding how the "X" should be pronounced.

Eu fui **à** escola," "to" and "the" are contracted in Portuguese, and together they produce "à," which is pronounced with an open sound. The grave accent is only used above the vowel "a."

When it comes to consonants, the only diacritical mark used is the cedilla, and only under the "c." Its effect is to change the usual hard sound to a soft one, much like the "s" in the English word "soccer." E.g.: Coçar (to scratch); Raça (race).

However, also as established in the previous sub-chapter, diacritics not only change the sound of the letter but also signal the syllable on which the tonic accent is:

| English | Portuguese |
|---|---|
| Criticism | **Crí**-ti-ca |
| Holiday | **Fé**-ri-as |
| Legendary | Len-**dá**-ri-o |
| Sympathetic | Sim-**pá**-ti-co |

What about when words don't have an accent mark – in which syllable does the stress fall then? The rule is that when there is no diacritic, the tonic accent falls on the penultimate syllable of the word:

| English | Portuguese |
|---|---|
| Accent | A-**cen**-to |
| Acute | A-**gu**-do |
| Circumflex | Cir-cum-**fle**-xo |
| Criticizes | Cri-**ti**-ca |

| Sympathy | Sim-pa-**ti**-a |
|---|---|

Even though that was the rule, there are, as always, exceptions to it. So, whenever a word ends with an "I," an "L," a "R," a "Z," "UM," "UNS," "IM," and "INS," the stress of the word should be in the last syllable instead. Like this:

| **English** | **Portuguese** |
|---|---|
| (I) seduced | (Eu) se-du-**zi** |
| Diagonal | Di-a-go-**nal** |
| (To) Exercise | Ex-er-ci-**tar** |
| Licorice | Al-ca-**çuz** |
| Common | Co-**mum** |
| Langoustines | La-gos-**tins** |
| Uncommon | In-co-**muns** |
| Dressing Room | Ca-ma-**rim** |

At this point, you should be able to read aloud the alphabet with a correct Portuguese accent with the little tips provided in the table below:

| A | á |
|---|---|
| B | bê |
| C | cê |

| | |
|---|---|
| D | dê |
| E | é |
| F | éfe |
| G | guê |
| H | hagá |
| I | í |
| J | jota |
| K | kápa |
| L | éle |
| M | éme |
| N | éne |
| O | ó |
| P | pê |
| Q | quê |
| R | érre |
| S | ésse |
| T | tê |

| | |
|---|---|
| U | ú |
| V | vê |
| W | dabliú |
| X | xíz |
| Y | ípsilon |
| Z | zê |

# 1.4 Word Order

In order to brush up on your grammar, let's quickly review and define a few classes of words before jumping into how to order them in a sentence. There are, in total, ten classes of words in the Portuguese language; for now, we will focus, however, only on pronouns, nouns, adjectives, verbs, adverbs, conjunctions, and prepositions.

**Nouns**, or substantives, are a class of words used to designate or name beings – people, animals, and things.

**Pronouns** exist to substitute or represent the nouns or names in a sentence. There are six types of pronouns – personal, demonstrative; possessive, relative; interrogative, and indefinite. The use of pronouns prevents your speech or writing from becoming too repetitive, thus making the conversation flow more seamlessly.

**Adjectives** are used to attribute traits or characteristics to nouns. They give the interlocutor more information about the person, animal, or thing that is being talked about.

**Verbs** are basically action descriptors – they indicate and inform about events represented in time.

While **adverbs** never modify a noun, this word class functions as an information provider about the verb – it can modify or characterize an action – further explaining how the verbal action is occurring. It can also modify the adjective or another adverb.

**Prepositions** are a word class that serves as the connection of the meaning within a sentence. Their main function is to establish a bridge between two parts of a phrase that are dependent on each other to make sense.

**Conjunctions**, much like prepositions, are bridges between the elements of a sentence. However, these two parts of the sentence are not dependent on each other to make sense, *i.e.,* they could be in an independent phrase and still make sense. They can either be coordinating or subordinating conjunctions.

Now, moving on to the order of the words in Portuguese. The good news is that the order of words in sentences is very much alike in both Portuguese and English, which makes things easier. There are some exceptions, but we'll get there.

First things first: in a declarative statement, just like in English, it goes 1) SUBJECT + 2) VERB + 3) OBJECT / COMPLEMENT (when there is one).

| I eat bread. | Eu como pão. |
|---|---|
| He drinks water. | Ele bebe água. |
| You are men. | Vocês são homens. |

However, in descriptive sentences, the adjective usually follows the noun instead of preceding it like it sometimes does in English:

| Your **yellow** car is broken. | O teu carro **amarelo** está partido. |
|---|---|
| He is a **big** man. | Ele é um homem **grande**. |
| They have a **small** house. | Eles têm uma casa **pequena**. |

In negative statements, the word "NÃO (not)" is placed before the verb, and that's enough to turn an affirmative statement into a negative one.

| English | PT - affirmative | PT - negative |
|---|---|---|
| I like you. | Eu gosto de ti. | Eu **não** gosto de ti. |
| She stole my bike. | Ela roubou a minha bicicleta. | Ela **não** roubou a minha bicicleta. |

In interrogative statements, unlike in English, there is no need to switch the order between the subject and the verb. A statement turns into a question by merely adding a question mark at the end of a sentence and rising the intonation of the phrase.

| | |
|---|---|
| The ball is yours. | A bola é tua. |
| Is the ball yours? | A bola é tua? |
| They are running. | Eles estão a correr. |
| Are they running? | Eles estão a correr? |

# 1.5 Capitalization and Punctuation

Regarding the rules of capitalization, the following are the situations in which uppercase should be used:

– Acronyms;

– Beginning of a sentence;

– Book titles;

– Cardinal points and their abbreviations;

– Geographical names, such as countries, streets, rivers, and mountains;

– Historical facts;

– Holidays and festive activities;

– Honorific titles;

- Months;
- Names of fictitious characters;
- Names of institutions, institutes, organizations, and associations;
- Names of populations, races, tribes, castes, religious entities, and their beliefs;
- Proper nouns;
- Pronouns referring to a god;
- Seasons of the year.

Lowercase should be used in every other situation where the rule of capitalization doesn't apply, plus also when:

- Using everyday vocabulary;
- Referring to the days of the week;
- Writing about geographical terms, such as "river" or "mountain," when used before the name of the river or mountain itself;
- Names of populations when used as adjectives.

When it comes to punctuation, which is used, as you know, to convey pause and intonation within sentences, the same rules that are used in the English language also apply to the Portuguese idiom, with a few exceptions. For instance, the apostrophe is used in the English language to indicate possession, whereas in Portuguese, there are specific words for that end. Moreover, in English, the apostrophe is also used in contractions, whereas in Portuguese, it is very rare to see it used to show the contraction of words[11]. Finally, the apostrophe is used in English to form the plural of letters, whereas, in Portuguese, the plural is indicated by the article or number that precedes the noun.

---

[11] The apostrophe in Portuguese contractions is used when, for instance, a movie title that begins with a definite article is preceded by the preposition "de." *E.g.*: Tenho uma t-shirt d' O Padrinho. (I have a t-shirt from The Godfather.) Since the "O (the)" is part of the name of the movie, the word doesn't merge with the preceding preposition.

The other relevant difference pertains to the usage of commas when writing the date. In Portuguese, no commas are needed to separate dates, unlike in English.

Lastly, due to the many similarities between Portuguese and Spanish and just so that no confusion arises, it may be worth noting that even though in Spain, the beginning of an interrogative sentence starts with an inverted question mark, as well as ending with a regular one, in Portuguese, the question mark is used just like it is in the English language, meaning, only at the end of a question.

| English | Portuguese |
|---|---|
| It is Mary's. | É **da** Maria. |
| Let's go. | *No equivalent*[12] |
| 2 M's | 2 (dois) M |
| April 13th, 2022 | 13 de Abril de 2022 |
| What is your name? | Qual é o teu nome?[13] |

# 1.6 Colors

On to more colorful subjects! You can learn how to state your favorite, second favorite, and third favorite colors in Portuguese - in case anybody is interested!

---

[12] Although it has no contraction equivalent, this could be translated to something like "Vamos embora."

[13] In Spanish, in the beginning there would be an upside-down question mark: ¿Como te llamas?

| English | Portuguese |
|---------|------------|
| Beige | Bege |
| Black | Preto |
| Blue | Azul |
| Brown | Castanho |
| Burgundy | Bordô[14] |
| Gold | Dourado |
| Gray | Cinzento |
| Green | Verde |
| Orange | Cor-de-laranja[15] |
| Pink | Cor-de-rosa[16] |
| Purple | Roxo |
| Red | Vermelho |
| Silver | Prateado |

[14] Keep in mind that burgundy can also written as "Bordeaux."

[15] This literally means "color of the orange."

[16] This translation, like the one before, literally means "color of the rose." A rose, as you're surely know, has several different colors, one of them being pink – hence the name.

| | |
|---|---|
| Turquoise | Turquesa |
| White | Branco |
| Yellow | Amarelo |

# 1.7 Numbers: 0 to 20

The Latin alphabet isn't the only thing the English language shares with the Portuguese. When it comes to numbers, Arabic numerals are also used in both idioms. However, the written forms differ. Check out how to write from 0 up to 20 in Portuguese.

| English | Portuguese |
|---|---|
| Zero | Zero |
| One | Um |
| Two | Dois |
| Three | Três |
| Four | Quatro |
| Five | Cinco |
| Six | Seis |
| Seven | Sete |
| Eight | Oito |
| Nine | Nove |

| | |
|---|---|
| Ten | Dez |
| Eleven | Onze |
| Twelve | Doze |
| Thirteen | Treze |
| Fourteen | Catorze |
| Fifteen | Quinze |
| Sixteen | Dezasseis |
| Seventeen | Dezassete |
| Eighteen | Dezoito |
| Nineteen | Dezanove |
| Twenty | Vinte |

# 1.8 Is it different in Brazil?

As mentioned previously, there are many countries that have Portuguese as their official language, and even though the language is almost the same, there are many differences between all of these variants. Actually, just like in any other language, there are different expressions, words, accents, and intonations, which vary from region to region within the same country.

However, Brazil is the country with the highest number of native speakers in the world. The reason a rapidly growing number of people want to learn Portuguese is due to the economic potential of Brazil, so it may be especially useful to at least understand the particular differences since it is becoming more pervasive than its

European counterpart.

To start with, the accent is different; not to worry, though – the differences in pronunciation may be compared to the differences between British English and American English. There are different words, expressions, and pronunciations, but everyone that speaks English understands both accents just fine (provided their accent is not super heavy).

There are some differences in the structuring of sentences, such as word order for instance, which may be worth mentioning, so you're not caught off guard when or if you end up talking to a Brazilian.

Let's start with how Brazilians structure informal speech *versus* how the Portuguese do it.

When talking to someone informally, Portuguese use the second-person singular and the personal pronoun "tu." Brazilians, however, used the word "você," and conjugate the verb in the third-person singular. Check out the following sentences to see how it all plays out:

| English | European PT | Brazilian PT |
|---|---|---|
| Are you my friend? | **Tu** és meu amigo? | **Você** é meu amigo? |
| You don't know anything! | **Tu** não sabes nada! | **Você** não sabe nada! |

Another difference has to do with the placement of the reflexive pronouns in a phrase. If in European Portuguese the reflexive pronoun appears typically after the verb, in Brazilian Portuguese, the pronoun is more often than not placed before the verb. For instance:

| English | European PT | Brazilian PT |
|---|---|---|
| I'm going to leave. | Eu vou-**me** embora. | Eu **me** vou embora. |
| He felt bad. | Ele sentiu-**se** mal. | Ele **se** sentiu mal. |
| You complimented me. | Vocês elogiaram-**me**. | Vocês **me** elogiaram. |

When it comes to describing actions in the present moment, Brazilians usually prefer the gerund of a verb, whereas in Portugal, the infinitive is used. Take, for instance, the sentences used in the previously table, now adapted to actions occurring in the present moment:

| English | European PT | Brazilian PT |
|---|---|---|
| I'm leaving. | Eu estou a **ir**-me embora. | Eu me estou **indo** embora. |
| He's feeling bad. | Ele está a **sentir**-se mal. | Ele se está **sentindo** mal. |
| You're complimenting me. | Vocês estão a **elogiar**-me. | Vocês me estão **elogiando**. |

Finally, in Brazilian Portuguese, there are also a lot of day-to-day words that differ slightly from European Portuguese. Most Brazilians and Portuguese have enough exposure to both cultures to understand each other perfectly; to a beginner, however, things might appear a tad confusing at times.

As a good opportunity for your vocabulary to become even more versatile, here is a table with a few words that are different in these two countries:

| English | European PT | Brazilian PT |
|---|---|---|
| Bathroom | Casa de banho | Banheiro |
| Breakfast | Pequeno-almoço | Café da manhã |
| Bus | Autocarro | Ônibus |
| Cellphone | Telemóvel | Celular |
| Fridge | Frigorífico | Geladeira |
| (Giving a) ride | (Dar) boleia | (Dar) carona |
| Grass | Relva | Gramado |
| Ice cream | Gelado | Sorvete |
| Thing | Coisa | Negócio |
| Juice | Sumo | Suco |
| Money | Dinheiro | Grana |
| Nap | Sesta | Cochilo |
| Ok | Ok | Valeu |
| Toilet seat | Sanita | Vaso |
| Train | Comboio | Trem |
| Tram | Eléctrico | Bonde |

| | | |
|---|---|---|
| Truck | Camião | Caminhão |
| Under panties | Cuecas | Calcinha |
| Gym | Ginásio | Academia |

# Chapter 2: Meeting New People

« *That was a great start! I'm now ready to move on to and learn more about Portuguese! But how? I now know that Portuguese is a rich and complex language that needs a great deal of dedication. Well, it's true that they say that the best way to learn a language is to be fully immersed in it, so I guess I'll just strike up a conversation with a native and see where it leads me!* »

*"Hi there! Are you Portuguese? Sorry to bother you, but I'm heading to Lisbon with no clue on how to speak Portuguese. Would you mind teaching me a thing or two about the language?*

*"Hello! And yes, I am. No problem! We will start with greetings and introductions and then I'll explain you how to say the* **subject pronouns** *in Portuguese, how to* **conjugate the verb "to be in the present tense**,*" which might just be the most common and important one, and how the* **gender of nouns** *work. That should be enough to get you going through these initial stages."*

# 2.1 Greetings & Introductions

Let's kick it off with a typical dialogue based on some simple questions to get to know someone else:

- *Bom dia! Eu sou o Tom. Como te chamas?* (*Good morning! I'm Tom. What is your name?*)

- *Olá, Tom. Eu sou o João. Como estás?* (*Hi, Tom. I'm João. How are you?*)

- *Bem, obrigado[17]. E tu?* (*Good, thanks. And you?*)

- *Está tudo bem, obrigado. Que idade tens?* (*Everything is okay, thank you. How old are you?*)

- *Tenho 31 anos. De onde és?* (*I'm thirty-one years old. Where are you from?*)

- *Eu sou de Lisboa. E tu? Qual é a tua nacionalidade?* (*I'm from Lisbon. And you? What is your nationality?*)

---

[17] There is a little detail regarding thanking somebody that you should pay attention to: if you're a man, you should say "Obrigad<u>o</u>"; if you're a woman, you should say "Obrigad<u>a</u>." The gender of the person you are speaking to is irrelevant. In this case, since the person saying it was a man – John – he should say, as he did, "Obrigado."

*- Eu sou um Americano de Nova Iorque. Bem, obrigado pela tua ajuda. (I'm an American from New York. Well, thank you for your help.)*

*- De nada! (You're welcome!)*

That's how a basic conversation would go. But just like in English, there are many ways to greet somebody and introduce yourself.

| English | Portuguese |
|---|---|
| Good morning! | Bom dia! |
| Good afternoon! | Boa tarde! |
| Good night/ evening! | Boa noite! |
| Good morning, afternoon, or evening! | Boas![18] |
| Hello/ Hi! | Olá! |
| Welcome to Portugal. | Bem-vindo a Portugal. |
| How are you feeling today? | Como te sentes hoje? |

[18] An abbreviation of "Boas manhãs/tardes/noites." Just keep in mind that it's a very informal way to greet somebody.

| | |
|---|---|
| Well, thanks. | Bem, obrigado/a. |
| Is everything ok? | Está tudo bem? |
| Everything is fine. | Está tudo bem. |
| How are you? | Como estás? |
| I'm great. | Estou bem. |
| How are you doing? | Como tens passado? |
| I'm doing fine. | Tenho passado bem. |
| You look nice. | Estás bonito/a.[19] |
| You're welcome. | De nada. |
| Pleasure to meet you. | Prazer em conhecer-te. |
| And you too. | E a ti também. |
| Have a nice day. | Resto de um bom dia. |
| See you later. | Até logo. |
| See you soon. | Até já. |
| Goodbye. | Adeus. |

[19] The gender of adjectives will be approached in an upcoming chapter – for now, just keep in mind that when characterizing someone, the word chosen must agree with the gender of the person that is being described.

| | |
|---|---|
| Thank you for your help. | Obrigado/a pela tua ajuda. |
| I'm grateful. | Agradecido/a. |
| What is your name? | Qual é o teu nome? |
| What's your name? (Literally, "How are you called?") | Como te chamas? |
| My name is ... | O meu nome é... |
| I'm called ... | Eu chamo-me... |
| Where do you live? | Onde vives? |
| I live in Coimbra. | Eu vivo em Coimbra. |
| How old are you? | Que idade tens? / Quantos anos tens? |
| I'm 47 years old. | Tenho 47 anos. |
| Where are you from? | De onde és? |
| I'm from California. | Eu sou da California. |
| What is your nationality? | Qual é a tua nacionalidade? |
| I'm Brazilian. | Sou Brasileiro/a. |

# 2.2 Grammar

### 2.2.1 Subject Pronouns

As for the grammar, let's start with subject pronouns since they are the most important and the ones that are more commonly used, both in speaking and writing. They work exactly like pronouns do in English: you just have to substitute the noun for the corresponding pronoun.

| English | Portuguese |
| --- | --- |
| I | Eu |
| You | Tu |
| He / She / It | Ele / Ela |
| We | Nós |
| You | Vós |
| They | Eles / Elas |

### 2.2.2 Verb "To Be"

The verb "to be" in Portuguese is actually a bit tricky because there are two verbs that can translate to this verb: the verbs "Ser" and "Estar."

The difference between them is that the verb "Ser" is usually the chosen one when it comes to talking about states that tend to be continuous and/or long-lasting throughout your lifetime. For instance, when identifying your nationality, gender, personality trait, or what the day of the week is, you should use the verb "Ser." *E.g.:*

"I am ambitious." – "Eu **_sou_** ambicioso."

"You are a woman." – "Tu **_és_** uma mulher."

"Today is Thursday." – Hoje **_é_** quinta-feira."

| Verbo SER | |
|---|---|
| Eu | Sou |
| Tu | És |
| Ele/a | É |
| Nós | Somos |
| Vós | Sois |
| Eles/as | São |

On the contrary, the verb "Estar" is used to refer to states that tend to be susceptible to changes. As an example, statements about how somebody is feeling at a specific time or about the weather or temperature should be constructed with the verb "Estar." *E.g.:*

"He is tired." – "Ele **_está_** cansado."

"It is cold in here." – "**_Está_** frio aqui."

"They are there." – Eles **estão** ali."

| Verbo ESTAR | |
|---|---|
| Eu | Estou |
| Tu | Estás |
| Ele/a | Está |
| Nós | Estamos |
| Vós | Estais |

| Eles/as | Estão |
|---|---|

### 2.2.3 Gender of nouns

Unlike the English language, which typically has no distinction between masculine and feminine nouns, Portuguese nouns always have a gender. Consequently, most of the time, nouns are variable, meaning that they change according to gender. They can vary when they are referring to people or animals (not objects), even though there are some nouns that are unisex[20], meaning they have only one form.

To start, you should know that masculine is usually the default and that the most common indication that a noun is masculine is if it ends with an "O." As to feminine nouns, they normally end with an "A." However, as with every rule, this too is full of exceptions, since that are nouns that end with an "A" that are masculine, *e.g.*, "Dilema (dilemma)," "Sofá (sofa), or "Cinema (cinema)."

To change the gender of a noun that ends with an "O" to feminine (or vice-versa), you usually just need to swap it for an "A." Like this:

| **English** | **Masculine** | **Feminine** |
|---|---|---|
| Boyfriend/girlfriend | Namorad**o** | Namorad**a** |
| Cat | Gat**o** | Gat**a** |
| Cousin | Prim**o** | Prim**a** |
| Friend | Amig**o** | Amig**a** |

However, there are many words that have different endings. Even though the following cases have several exceptions, these are

20 There are unisex nouns, which we will cover later on on this book.

some guidelines you should follow when in doubt.

### Nouns ending in "ÃO":

When it comes to nouns ending with the diphthong "ÃO," they are usually masculine. To change it to feminine, there are usually three possible suffix modifications:

- The "O" drops;
- The "ÃO" turns into "OA";
- The "ÃO" turns into "ONA."

Let's see some examples:

| English | Masculine | Feminine |
|---|---|---|
| Captain | Capit**ão** | Capit**ã** |
| Surgeon | Cirurgi**ão** | Cirurgi**ã** |
| Lion / Lioness | Le**ão** | Le**oa** |
| Boss | Patr**ão** | Patr**oa** |
| Glutton | Glut**ão** | Gluto**na** |
| Reveler | Foli**ão** | Foli**ona** |

### Nouns ending in "OR":

When nouns end with "OR," they are almost always masculine and turn into feminine by *adding* the letter "A."

| English | Masculine | Feminine |
|---|---|---|
| Driver | Condut**or** | Condut**ora** |
| Seller | Vended**or** | Vended**ora** |

| Sir | Senh**or** | Senh**ora** |

## Nouns ending in "E":

Nouns ending with an "E" just need to *switch* it to an "A" to change the gender of the word. Like this:

| English | Masculine | Feminine |
| --- | --- | --- |
| Governor | Governant**e** | Governant**a** |
| Master | Mestr**e** | Mestr**a** |
| Prince / Princess (that are not heirs to the throne)[21] | Infant**e** | Infant**a** |

## Nouns ending in "EU":

With nouns ending in "EU," the feminine is formed by *swapping* those with the letters "EIA." For example:

| English | Masculine | Feminine |
| --- | --- | --- |
| Commoner | Pleb**eu** | Pleb**eia** |
| European | Europ**eu** | Europ**eia** |
| Pigmee | Pigm**eu** | Pigm**eia** |

## Nouns ending in "ÊS":

With nouns ending in "ÊS," the feminine is formed by *adding* the letter "A" to the end of the word and dropping the circumflex

---

[21] If they were heirs to the throne, the translation to Portuguese would be "Prince – Príncipe" and "Princess – Princesa."

mark. For example:

| English | Masculine | Feminine |
|---------|-----------|----------|
| Customer | Freguês | Freguesa |
| Marquis | Marquês | Marquesa |
| Peasant | Camponês | Camponesa |

However, as mentioned earlier, there are a lot of exceptions to these rules, and there is no other way around it but to memorize them. Take a look at a collection of examples that are exceptions to the rules explained above:

| English | Masculine | Feminine |
|---------|-----------|----------|
| Husband / Wife | Marido | Mulher |
| Stepfather / Stepmother | Padrasto | Madrasta |
| Baron / Baroness | Barão | Baronesa |
| Dog | Cão | Cadela |
| Actor / Actress | Actor | Actriz |
| Emperor / Empress | Imperador | Imperatriz |
| Jew | Judeu | Judia |
| Defendant | Réu | Ré |
| Hero / Heroin | Herói | Heroína |

| Poet | Poeta | Poetisa |
|---|---|---|
| Prince / Princess | Príncipe | Princesa |
| King / Queen | Rei | Rainha |

# 2.3 Vocabulary

## 2.3.2 Countries and Nationalities

Below, you will find a list of several countries and their respective nationalities. You will also see displayed the phonetic transcription in both European and Brazilian Portuguese. To help you read the phonetic notation, there is a chart at the end of this book that lists out all of the graphemes and how they should be read.

| Country | Nationality | European PT | Brazilian PT |
|---|---|---|---|
| Afghanistan – Afeganistão | Afegão | ɐ.fɨ.ˈgẽw | afeˈgẽw |
| Argentina – Argentina | Argentino | ɐɾ.ʒẽ.ˈti.nu | aʁʒẽˈtʃinu |
| Australia – Austrália | Australiano | awʃ.tɾɐ.łi.ˈɐ.nu | awʃtɾaliˈɐnu |
| Belarus – Bielorrússia | Bielorrusso | bɨ.i.łu.ˈʁu.zu | bie.lo.ˈɾu.su |
| Belgium – Bélgica | Belga | ˈbɛł.gɐ | ˈbɛw.gɐ |
| Brazil – Brasil | Brasileiro | bɾɐ.zi.ˈłɐj.ɾu | bɾa.zi.ˈlej.ɾu |

| | | | |
|---|---|---|---|
| Canada – Canadá | Canadense | kɐ.nɐ.di.ˈɐ.nɐ | kɐ.na.dʒi.ˈɐ.nɐ |
| Cape Verde – Cabo Verde | Cabo-verdiano | ˈka.bu-viɾ.di.ˈɐ.nu | ka.bo.veʁ.dʒi.ˈɐ.nu |
| China – China | Chinês | ʃi.ˈneʃ | ʃi.ˈneʃ |
| Colombia – Colômbia | Colombiano | ku.ɫõ.bi.ˈɐ.nu | ko.lõ.bi.ˈɐ.nu |
| Croatia – Croácia | Croata | kɾu.ˈa.tɐ | kɾo.ˈa.tɐ |
| Denmark – Dinamarca | Dinamarquês | di.nɐ.maɾ.ˈkeʃ | dʒi.nɐ.maʁ.ˈkeʃ |
| East Timor – Timor-Leste | Timorense | ti.mu.ˈrẽ.sɨ | tʃi.mo.ˈrẽ.si |
| Ecuador – Equador | Equatoriano | i.kwɐ.tu.ɾi.ˈɐ.nu | i.kwa.to.ɾi.ˈɐ.nu |
| Egypt – Egipto | Egípcio | i.ˈgip.sɨ.u | i.ˈʒip.siu |
| England – Inglaterra | Inglês | ĩ.ˈgɫeʃ | ĩ.ˈgleʃ |
| France – França | Francês | fɾẽ.ˈseʃ | fɾẽ.ˈseʃ |
| Germany – Alemanha | Alemão | ɐ.lɨ.ˈmẽw | a.le.ˈmẽw |

| | | | |
|---|---|---|---|
| Greece – Grécia | Grego | ˈgɾe.gu | ˈgɾɛ.gu |
| Guinea-Bissau – Guiné-Bissau | Guineense | gi.nɨ.ˈẽ.sɨ | gj.ne.ˈẽ.si |
| India – Índia | Indiano[22] | ĩ.dɨ.ˈɐ.nu | ĩ.dʒi.ˈɐ.nu |
| Iran – Irão | Iraniano | i.ɾɐ.ni.ˈɐ.nu | i.ɾɐ.ni.ˈɐ.nu |
| Iraq – Iraque | Iraquiano | i.ɾɐ.ki.ˈɐ.nu | i.ɾa.ki.ˈɐ.nu |
| Ireland – Irlanda | Irlandês | iɾ.ɫẽ.ˈdeʃ | iʁ.lẽ.ˈdeʃ |
| Italy – Itália | Italiano | i.tɐ.ɫi.ˈɐ.nu | i.ta.li.ˈɐ.nu |
| Japan – Japão | Japonês | ʒɐ.pu.ˈneʃ | ʒa.po.ˈneʃ |
| Mexico – México | Mexicano | mɨ.ʃi.ˈkɐ.nu | me.ʃi.ˈkɐ.nu |
| Morocco – Marrocos | Marroquino | ma.ʁu.ˈki.nu | ma.ʁo.ˈki.nu |
| Mozambique – Moçambique | Moçambicano | mu.sẽ.bi.ˈkɐ.nu | mo.sẽ.bi.ˈkɐ.nu |
| Netherlands – Holanda | Holandês | o.ɫẽ.ˈdeʃ | o.lẽ.ˈdeʃ |

---

[22] You might come across the word "Índio" or "Índia," which is very similar to this one but translates to native American.

| | | | |
|---|---|---|---|
| New Zealand - Nova Zelândia | Neozelandês | ni.u.zɨ.ɫẽ.ˈdeʃ | nio.ze.lẽ.ˈdeʃ |
| Nigeria - Nigéria | Nigeriano | nɨ.ʒɨ.ɾi.ˈɐ.nu | ni.ʒe.ɾi.ˈɐ.nu |
| North Korea - Coreia do Norte | Norte-coreano | ˈnoɾ.tɨ-ku.ɾi.ˈɐ.nu | noʁ.te.ko.ɾi.ˈɐ.nu |
| Paraguay - Paraguai | Paraguaio | pɐ.ɾɐ.gwaj.u | pa.ɾa.ˈgwaju |
| Russia - Rússia | Russo | ˈʁu.su | ˈʁu.su |
| São Tomé and Príncipe - São Tomé e Príncipe | São-tomense | ˈsẽw-tu.ˈmẽ.sɨ | ˈsẽw.tu.mẽ.si |
| Saudi Arabia - Arábia Saudita | Saudita | saw.ˈdi.tɐ | saw.ˈdʒi.tɐ |
| Scotland - Escócia | Escocês | ʃ.ku.ˈseʃ | iʃ.ko.ˈseʃ |
| Serbia - Sérvia | Sérvio | ˈsɛɾ.vi.u | ˈsɛʁ.viu |
| South Africa - África do Sul | Sul-africano | ˈsuɫ-ɐ.fri.ˈkɐ.nu | suwa.fri.ˈkɐ.nu |
| South Korea - Coreia do Sul | Sul-coreano | ˈsuɫ-ku.ɾi.ˈɐ.nu | suw.ko.ɾi.ˈɐ.nu |

| | | | |
|---|---|---|---|
| Spain – Espanha | Espanhol | ʃ.pɐ.ˈɲɔɫ | iʃ.pɐ.ˈɲɔw |
| Sweden – Suécia | Sueco | su.ˈe.ku | su.ˈɛ.ku |
| Switzerland – Suíça | Suíço | su.ˈi.su | su.ˈi.su |
| Turkey – Turquia | Turco | ˈtuɾ.ku | ˈtuʁ.ku |
| Ukraine – Ucrânia | Ucraniano | u.kɾɐ.ni.ˈɐ.nu | u.kɾɐ.ni.ˈɐ.nu |
| United States of America – Estados Unidos da América | Americano | ɐ.mɨ.ɾi.ˈkɐ.nu | ɐ.me.ɾi.ˈkɐ.nu |
| Uruguay – Uruguai | Uruguaio | u.ɾu.ˈgwaj.u | u.ɾu.ˈgaju |
| Venezuela – Venezuela | Venezuelano | vɨ.nɨ.zu.i.ˈlɐ.nu | ve.ne.zue.ˈlɐ.nu |

## 2.3.3 Numbers over 20

Now, let's learn about cardinal numbers from 20 and up.

| English | Portuguese |
|---|---|
| Twenty | Vinte |
| Thirty | Trinta |

| English | Portuguese |
|---|---|
| Forty | Quarenta |
| Fifty | Cinquenta |
| Sixty | Sessenta |
| Seventy | Setenta |
| Eighty | Oitenta |
| Ninety | Noventa |
| One hundred | Cem |

You might have noticed that the table omitted the numbers between each set of ten. That is because every number between each set of ten adopts the same rule – much like in English, you merely add the required number at the end. The only difference is that an "and" is also added between the two numbers (the literal translation would be: "Twenty *and* six). Like this:

| English | Portuguese |
|---|---|
| Fifty-three | Cinquenta e *três* |
| Sixty-seven | Sessenta e *sete* |
| Seventy-nine | Noventa e *nove* |
| Eight-two | Oitenta e *dois* |
| Ninety-one | Noventa e *um* |

# 2.4 Exercises

Now it is time to practice! Don't fret, though – at the end of the book, you can find the solution to all of the exercises in this and the following chapters.

1) Underline the subject pronouns and different forms of the verb "to be" in the dialogue found at the beginning of the chapter.

2) Rewrite all of the nationalities in the feminine form.

| Masculine | Feminine | Masculine | Feminine |
|---|---|---|---|
| Afegão | | Iraquiano | |
| Alemão | | Irlandês | |
| Americano | | Italiano | |
| Argentino | | Japonês | |
| Australiano | | Marroquino | |
| Belga | | Mexicano | |
| Bielorrusso | | Moçambicano | |
| Brasileiro | | Neozelandês | |
| Cabo-verdiano | | Neozelandês | |
| Canadiano | | Nigeriano | |
| Chinês | | Norte-coreano | |

| | | | |
|---|---|---|---|
| Colombiano | | Paraguaio | |
| Croata | | Russo | |
| Dinamarquês | | São-tomense | |
| Egípcio | | Saudita | |
| Equatoriano | | Sérvio | |
| Escocês | | Sueco | |
| Espanhol | | Suíço | |
| Francês | | Sul-africano | |
| Grego | | Sul-coreano | |
| Guineense | | Timorense | |
| Holandês | | Turco | |
| Indiano | | Ucraniano | |
| Inglês | | Uruguaio | |
| Iraniano | | Venezuelano | |

3) Imagine Tom struck up a conversation with another passenger. Write down the dialogue between them using what you have learned up until now.

# Chapter 3: Checking into the Hotel

« *That was amazing! I hope it is enough for me to be able to check into my hotel room. Maybe I can even learn how to do it in Portuguese – let's just hope the hotel clerk is just as nice as my last "professor"!* »

"*Olá! I wanted to book a room and check-in, please. Just wanted to ask something first: would you mind translating to Portuguese whatever I ask in English just so that I can learn? I'll be taking notes!*"

"*Boa tarde! Yes sure. Oh, and hey: at the hotel gift shop we have this book "An introduction to Portuguese" that touches on some basic grammar as well, such as* **definite and indefinite articles, yes and no questions, and prepositions of place.** *It might be worth giving it a read!*"

# 3.1 Booking a room & checking-in

So, let's check out an example dialogue of how booking a room and checking in would look like:

*- Boa tarde. Gostaria de reservar um quarto com vista para o oceano por 7 noites, por favor. (Good afternoon. I would like to book a room with an ocean view for 7 nights, please.)*

*- Com certeza. Quarto individual, de casal ou com duas camas? (Sure. Single, double, or twin room?)*

*- Uma suíte na verdade, se for possível. Equipada com minibar. (A suite, actually, if possible. Equipped with a mini bar.)*

*- Temos uma suíte disponível, mas é para não-fumadores. Tem acesso a serviço de quarto 24 horas, sinal de wi-fi forte e serviço de despertador. A diária é de 50€ por noite. (We have an available suite, but it's for non-smokers. It has access to 24 hours room service, strong wi-fi signal and wake-up call. The rate is of 50€ per night.)*

*- Perfeito. A que horas é o check-in? (Perfect. At what time is the check-in?)*

*- O check-in é às 12 horas. Mas somos bastantes flexíveis com o horário. (Check-in is at 12 p.m. But we are pretty flexible with the schedule.)*

*- Obrigada por tudo. Até então! (Thank you for everything. See you then!)*

# 3.2 Grammar

## 3.2.1 Definite & indefinite articles

First things first: what are articles? Articles, also otherwise known as determinants, are a class of words that come before nouns and are used to define their gender and number. There can either be definite or indefinite articles.

### Definite articles

Definite articles indicate defined or specific people, objects, and things. It is, as the name *determinant* implies, something that is determined or specified already. While in English there is only "THE," in Portuguese, there are singular and plural forms, as well as masculine and feminine forms. Take a look at the following examples:

- **O** prim**o**. (The [male] cousin.);
- **A** prim**a**. (The [female] cousin);
- **Os** ti**os**. (The uncles);
- **As** ti**as**. (The aunts).

Notice that the articles before the nouns are in accordance with the nouns' gender and number. This is crucial since sometimes, as was stated before, some nouns don't follow the rules, only being possible to identify its gender by the article (definite or indefinite) that precedes it.

## Indefinite articles

Indefinite articles imply that something is undetermined or unspecified. In English, there are two indefinite articles: "A" and "AN." In Portuguese, there are four, since they change according to gender and number, just like the definite articles. See how they are used in the sentences below:

  – **Um** prim<u>o</u>. (A [male] cousin);

  – **Uma** prim<u>a</u>. (A [female] cousin);

  – **Uns** ti<u>os</u>. (Some uncles);

  – **Umas** ti<u>as</u>. (Some aunts).

### 3.2.2 Yes & no questions

As you learned in the first chapter (1.4), in the Portuguese language, interrogative statements don't need the inversion between the subject and the verb - like in the English language. Usually, a descriptive sentence turns into a statement purely by adding a question mark to the end of the question and naturally rising the intonation of the voice while maintaining the exact same word order. That applies to simple questions – "yes or no questions" – of course, there are exceptions that we will talk about later on.

  – O jogo foi divertido. **O jogo foi divertido?** (The game was fun. Was the game fun?);

  – Tu comes muito rápido. **Tu comes muito rápido?** (You eat very fast. Do you eat very fast?);

  – Eles gostam de bacalhau. **Eles gostam de bacalhau?** (They like codfish. Do they like codfish?)

When it comes to answering these "yes or no questions," things are also quite straightforward. You can reply only with a simple "Sim. (Yes)" or "Não. (No)." However, answering with just one of these words by themselves might come across as a little harsh or rude. Instead, and just like in English, the answer usually contains repeated elements of the question, with the verb adapted to the speaker. Like this:

  – O jogo foi divertido? **Não, o jogo não foi divertido. / Não, não foi.** (No, the game wasn't fun. / No, it wasn't.);

– Tu comes muito rápido? **Sim, eu como muito rápido. /
Sim, como.** (Yes, I eat very fast. / Yes, I do.);

– Eles gostam de bacalhau? **Sim, eles gostam de bacalhau. /
Sim, gostam.** (Yes, they like codfish. / Yes, they do.)

### 3.2.3 Prepositions of place

As was stated previously, prepositions are a word class that
functions as the connection of the meaning within a sentence, *i.e.,*
two parts of a phrase are dependent on each other to make sense,
and the preposition connects them. More specifically, a preposition
of place establishes a relationship of space between the two
elements of a phrase. Let's get to know the most commonly used
*prepositions of place* in the Portuguese language:

| Preposições de lugar | |
|---|---|
| Above | Por cima |
| Around | Em volta de |
| At | Em |
| Behind of | Atrás de |
| Beside | Ao lado de |
| Between | Entre |
| Far from | Longe de |
| In front of | Na/em frente de |
| In the | No / na |
| Inside of | Dentro de |

| | |
|---|---|
| Near to / next to | Perto de |
| On | Em cima de |
| Outside of/out of | Fora de |
| Under | Debaixo de |

# 3.3 Vocabulary

### 3.3.1 Parts & rooms of the house

It's important that you know your way around in and outside of a house. Here's a vocabulary list that encompasses all you need to know about a home.

| English | Portuguese |
|---|---|
| Apartment | Apartamento |
| Attic | Sótão |
| Backyard | Quintal |
| Balcony | Varanda |
| Basement | Cave |
| Bathroom | Casa/quarto de banho |
| Bathtub | Banheira |
| Chimney | Chaminé |
| Closet | Armário |

| | |
|---|---|
| Corridor | Corredor |
| Dining room | Sala de jantar |
| Door | Porta |
| Garage | Garagem |
| Garden | Jardim |
| Guest room | Quarto de hóspedes |
| Hall | Hall de entrada |
| House | Casa |
| Kid's room | Quarto das crianças |
| Kitchen | Cozinha |
| Kitchen sink | Lava-loiça/louça |
| Laundry room | Lavandaria |
| Library | Biblioteca |
| Living room | Sala de estar |
| Nursery | Berçário |
| Office | Escritório |
| Pantry | Despensa |

| | |
|---|---|
| Roof | Telhado |
| Room, bedroom | Quarto |
| Sink | Lavatório |
| Stairs | Escadas |
| Toilet | Sanita |
| Utility/storeroom | Sala de arrumações |
| Window | Janela |
| Wine cellar | Adega |

### 3.3.3 Objects in the house

Ok, so maybe the last list wasn't all you needed to know about a home. But the following table for sure completes the intention. Check out a list of objects you may find inside a house.

| English | Portuguese |
|---|---|
| Backpack | Mochila |
| Bag | Saco |
| Bed | Cama |
| Book | Livro |
| Bottle | Garrafa |
| Bowl | Tigela |

| | |
|---|---|
| Candle | Vela |
| Clock | Relógio |
| Cradle/crib | Berço |
| Cup | Chávena |
| Cutlery | Talheres |
| Dishes | Pratos |
| Door lock | Fechadura da porta |
| Flashlight | Lanterna |
| Fork | Garfo |
| Furniture | Móveis |
| Glass (of water) | Copo |
| Glass (of a window) | Vidro |
| Knife | Faca |
| Lighter | Isqueiro |
| Magazines | Revistas |
| Matches | Fósforos |
| Mirror | Espelho |

| | |
|---|---|
| Napkin | Guardanapo |
| Newspaper | Jornal |
| Pen | Caneta |
| Pencil | Lápis |
| Plate | Prato |
| Pot | Panela |
| Scissors | Tesouras |
| Sleeping bag | Saco-cama |
| Sofa | Sofá |
| Spoon | Colher |
| Tablecloth | Toalha de mesa |
| Telephone | Telefone |
| Television | Televisão |
| Toilet paper | Papel higiénico |
| Toothbrush | Escova de dentes |
| Toothpaste | Pasta de dentes |
| Umbrella | Chapéu de chuva |

# 3.4 Exercises

1) Complete the following sentences with the correct definite or indefinite articles.

_O_ gato é preto. (The cat is black.)

Só ____ santos vão para o céu. (Only saints go to heaven.)

Esta é ___ namorada do meu irmão. (This is my brother's girlfriend.)

___ ruas estão vazias. (The streets are empty.)

2) Complete the following sentences with the correct indefinite articles.

Estão umas uvas na mesa. (There are some grapes on the table.)

Eu quero uma maçã. (I want an apple.)

Um americano falou comigo. (An American talked to me.)

Ele quer o ___ calções azuis. (He wants the blue shorts.)

3) Complete the following sentences using the correct prepositions of place.

A minha escola é _____ de casa. (My school is far away from home.)

A bola está _____ da caixa. (The ball is on the box.)

Eu vivo _____ da praia. (I live near the beach.)

Os talheres estão ____ despensa. (The cuttlery are in the pantry.)

Ele vive _____ da ponte. (He lives under the bridge.)

O relógio está _____ do sofá. (The clock is above the sofa.)

Está uma pessoa _____ de casa. (There is a person inside the house.)

4) Imagine you are Tom writing down in Portuguese a detailed description of all of the furniture and objects he might find in the different spaces of his hotel room. You can use the prepositions you have just learned about to better describe their location in the room.

# Chapter 4: Going Shopping

« All settled in and ready to go out and browse around! Maybe I can take a walk and buy some souvenirs to bring back home. That will give me a chance to show off my new Portuguese skills and maybe get to learn a bit more! This gift shop looks just right for it... »

"Boa tarde! I want to buy some souvenirs to take back home, but I'm also interested in learning Portuguese. Do you mind translating the sentences to Portuguese as I ask them?"

"Of course, it's no hassle at all. While we're at it, I might as well teach you some grammar. I guess I only have time to teach you about **demonstrative determiners**, **adverbs of quantity**, **interrogative pronouns**, and the **present form of regular verbs** before my shift ends. Let's get to it!

# 4.1 At the store

Let's begin then! You will see that roaming around a shop and asking about its products is pretty easy – it basically involves a lot of Wh-questions, which you just have to memorize, but you will surely do that in no time.

- *Boas! Quero comprar uma recordação para levar para casa. Pode ajudar-me, se faz favor?* (Good afternoon! I want to buy a souvenir to bring back home. Can you help, please?)

- *Claro! No que está a pensar? Para quem são os presentes?* (Of course. What are you thinking about? For whom are the gifts?)

- *São para a minha família. Eu gosto daquelas canecas. Esta t-shirt também é bonita. Quanto custa?* (They are for my family. I like those mugs. This t-shirt is also pretty. How much is it?)

- *Qual t-shirt? Esta aqui?* (Which t-shirt? This one right here?)

- *Essa mesmo.* (That's the one.)

- *Isto custa 8€.* (This costs 8€).

- *Está bem. Têm um tamanho maior?* (Ok. Do

*you have a bigger size?)*

*- Só temos tamanhos pequenos, desculpe. (We only have small sizes, sorry).*

*- Sem problema. Onde posso encontrar postais? (No problem. Where can I find postcards?)*

*- Isso está no corredor 6. (Those are on aisle 6).*

*- Muito obrigado! (Thank you very much!)*

In order to make it easier for you to study the Wh-questions, here is a table with all of them translated into Portuguese. Beware that some of the words belong to the adverbs class while others are considered pronouns. In the grammar section, we will again touch on some of the words that you have seen here – the interrogative pronouns – so don't be surprised by the repetition!

| English | Portuguese |
|---------|------------|
| What | Que |
| Who | Quem |
| Whose | De quem |
| Whom | Quem |
| When | Quando |
| Where | Onde |

| | |
|---|---|
| Why | Porquê |
| Which | Qual |
| How | Como |
| How long | Quanto |

# 4.2 Grammar

### 4.2.1 Demonstrative determiners

Demonstrative determiners indicate the position of an object in space. They play a crucial role in a sentence since they give information on where exactly an object is in relationship to the objects and space around it. The following is a list of all the demonstrative determiners in the Portuguese language:

| Determinantes demonstrativos | |
|---|---|
| This | Este / Esta |
| That | Esse / Essa |
| These | Estes / Estas |
| Those | Esses / Essas |
| That (located further away than "esse") | Aquele / Aquela |
| Those (located further away than "esses") | Aqueles / Aquelas |
| The other | O outro / A outra |

| The same | O mesmo / A mesma |
|---|---|
| This thing right here | Isto |
| That thing there (further away than "isto," but closer than "aquilo") | Isso |
| That thing over there | Aquilo |
| Such | Tal |

As a simple exercise, you can underline in the dialogue at the beginning of the chapter all the demonstrative determiners that you can find!

### 4.2.2 Adverbs of quantity

As we learned in the first chapter, adverbs function as an information provider about the verb, adjective, or another adverb, explaining in more detail how the action is occurring. Adverbs of quantity, in particular, express the degree or intensity with which the verbal action is occurring. Take a look at the following examples of adverbs of quantity:

| Advérbios de quantidade / intensidade ||
|---|---|
| A lot | Imenso / Imensa / Bastante |
| Almost | Quase |
| Least | Menos |
| Little | Pouco / Pouca |
| More / Further | Mais |

| Much / Very | Muito / Muita |
|---|---|
| Sufficiently | Suficientemente |
| Too | Demais |
| Too much | Demasiado |

To better understand how they work, let's see them in action:

- Isto é **demasiada** comida. (This is too much food.);
- Ele bebeu **pouco** vinho. (He drank little wine);
- Vocês dormem **imenso**. (You guys sleep a lot);
- Tu és **muito** forte! (You are very strong!)

### 4.2.3 Interrogative Pronouns

As you know, pronouns are used to substitute nouns. In this particular case, these pronouns are used to construct interrogative statements in a direct or indirect way. The questions themselves try to get even more information about a person or an object, and unlike the "yes or no questions," replying to them requires a bit more effort than a simple yes or no. The following are the interrogative pronouns in Portuguese:

| Pronomes interrogativos | |
|---|---|
| What | Que |
| Who | Quem |
| Which | Qual |
| Which | Quais |
| How much | Quanto / Quanta |

| How many | Quantos /Quantas |
|----------|------------------|

As a simple exercise, you can underline in the dialogue in the beginning of the chapter all the interrogative pronouns that you can find! But remember: only the interrogative pronouns and not all the Wh-questions!

### 4.2.4 Present tense of regular verbs

You already know what verbs are, but do you know what regular verbs are? Well, regular verbs are the ones that keep their stem constant throughout the whole process of conjugation – only the suffix changes. For instance, in the verb "INSISTIR (to insist)," "INSIST" is the stem, and "IR" is the suffix – the verb stem ends just before the last vowel of the verb in its infinitive form.

In Portuguese, there are three big classes of verbs: the ones ending with "AR," "ER," or "IR." When conjugating these verbs, assuming they are regular verbs, the last two letters drop and should be substituted by the same suffixes, time and time again.

Let's start by looking at the present tense of regular verbs ending in "AR." After the stem, you just need to add – "O," "AS," "A," "AMOS," "AIS," and "AM." For instance:

| Verbo AMAR (to love) ||
|-----------------------|-----------|
| Eu | Am**o** |
| Tu | Am**as** |
| Ele/a | Am**a** |
| Nós | Am**amos** |
| Vós | Am**ais** |
| Eles/as | Am**am** |

Now, as for the present tense of verbs ending in "ER." After the stem, you just need to add – "O," "ES," "E," "EMOS," "EIS," and "EM." For instance:

| Verbo VIVER (to live) | |
|---|---|
| Eu | Viv<u>o</u> |
| Tu | Viv<u>es</u> |
| Ele/a | Viv<u>e</u> |
| Nós | Viv<u>emos</u> |
| Vós | Viv<u>eis</u> |
| Eles/as | Viv<u>em</u> |

Finally, when it comes to the present tense of verbs ending in "IR." After the stem, you just need to add – "O," "ES," "E," "IMOS," "IS," and "EM." For instance:

| Verbo PARTIR (to break) | |
|---|---|
| Eu | Part<u>o</u> |
| Tu | Part<u>es</u> |
| Ele/a | Part<u>e</u> |
| Nós | Part<u>imos</u> |
| Vós | Part<u>is</u> |
| Eles/as | Part<u>em</u> |

# 4.3 Vocabulary

The following tables will help you write down your own shopping list!

## 4.3.1 Fruits & vegetables

| English | Portuguese |
|---------|------------|
| Apple | Maçã |
| Avocado | Abacate |
| Banana | Banana |
| Blackberry | Amora |
| Blueberry | Mirtilo |
| Broccoli | Brócolos |
| Cabbage | Couve |
| Carrot | Cenoura |
| Cherry | Cereja |
| Coconut | Côco |
| Cranberry | Arando |
| Eggplant | Beringela |
| Garlic | Alho |
| Gooseberry | Groselha |

| Grapes | Uvas |
|---|---|
| Leek | Alho Francês |
| Lemon | Limão |
| Lettuce | Alface |
| Lime | Lima |
| Mango | Manga |
| Mushroom | Cogumelo |
| Nuts | Nozes |
| Onion | Cebola |
| Orange | Laranja |
| Papaya | Papaia |
| Peach | Pêssego |
| Pear | Pêra |
| Pineapple | Ananás |
| Potato | Batata |
| Raspberry | Framboesa |
| Strawberries | Morangos |

| | |
|---|---|
| Sweet Potato | Batata doce |
| Tomato | Tomate |
| Vegetables | Vegetais |
| Zucchini | Courgette |

## 4.3.3 At the supermarket

| English | Portuguese |
|---|---|
| Barley | Cevada |
| Beef | Vaca |
| Beer | Cerveja |
| Butter | Manteiga |
| Cereal | Cereais |
| Bread | Pão |
| Fish | Peixe |
| Crackers | Bolachas |
| Sandwich | Sanduíche |
| Cheese | Queijo |
| Chocolate | Chocolate |

| | |
|---|---|
| Coffee | Café |
| Corn | Milho |
| Egg | Ovo |
| Flesh | Carne |
| Flour | Farinha |
| Ham | Fiambre |
| Ice cream | Gelado |
| Jam | Compota |
| Juice | Sumo |
| Meat | Carne |
| Milk | Leite |
| Oat | Aveia |
| Olive Oil | Azeite |
| Olives | Azeitonas |
| Peanut Butter | Manteiga de Amendoim |
| Peanuts | Amendoins |
| Pepper | Pimenta |

| | |
|---|---|
| Salt | Sal |
| Sausage | Salsicha |
| Sugar | Açúcar |
| Tea | Chá |
| Vinegar | Vinagre |
| Water | Água |
| Wine | Vinho |

# 4.4 Traditional Meals in Portugal & Brazil

Both Portuguese and Brazilian gastronomy is super rich, so it is time to check out a few traditional meals in Portugal and Brazil. There are some pictures next to the dishes, so your mouth can start watering! To kick it off, five typical Portuguese dishes.

### Bacalhau à Brás

In Portugal, it is often said that you can get a different dish of codfish for each day of the year. However, out of all of them, this might be the most famous. It is made with shredded codfish, grated potatoes, and mixed eggs.

**Bacalhau à Brás.**

*Avicentegil, CC BY-SA 4.0 <https://creativecommons.org/licenses/by-sa/4.0>, via Wikimedia Commons: https://commons.wikimedia.org/wiki/File:Bacalao_a_braz.jpg*

### Polvo à lagareiro

Octopus is also a typical ingredient of Portuguese cuisine. This particular meal consists of an oven-baked octopus with a lot of olive oil on top, which is then accompanied by roasted potatoes, garlic, paprika, and onion.

**Polvo à Lagareiro.**

### Cozido à Portuguesa

Literally, it means Portuguese stew, and even though it has many regional variations, it basically consists of a variety of boiled vegetables, meat, and sausages.

**Cozido à Portuguesa.**

### Francesinha

Literally meaning "little Frenchwoman," this famous sandwich was born in the city of Oporto. The recipe is made with bread slices, steak, sausages, and ham all covered in melting cheese and with a fried egg on top. The secret, however, is in the spicy sauce!

**Francesinha.**
*Jeremy Keith from Brighton & Hove, United Kingdom, CC BY 2.0*

## Amêijoas à Bulhão Pato

This ocean dish, which got its name from a Portuguese poet, consists of boiled clams with a touch of garlic, white wine, and coriander, which gives it its distinctive flavor. Lemon juice is added on top.

**Amêijoas à Bulhão Pato.**

## Feijoada

When it comes to Brazil's most traditional meal, this is undoubtedly number one. Being known and cooked in every village of this big country, this stew consists of black beans with different cuts of pork, accompanied by tomatoes, cabbage, and carrots. It is also served with fried kale mixed with small slices of bacon, white rice, and farofa.

Feijoada.

## Farofa

Farofa, which serves as a side dish to many Brazilian meals, ranging from the "feijoada," as we just saw, to barbecues, is toasted cassava flour, which has a characteristic salty and smoky flavor.

Farofa.

## Moqueca de Camarão

Moqueca is also a stew. Even though there are plenty of variations around the country, it usually is made with prawns or fish, coconut oil, and milk – with vegetables then added.

**Moqueca de camarão.**

# Empadão

Empadão is a pie with a chicken and vegetable mix filling. Sometimes, shrimp or other types of meat are used. It can either be served in small portions like the ones seen in the image, or in a larger tray.

**Empadão.**

# Picanha

Barbecues are big in Brazil, and "picanha" is the star of them all. It is a cut of beef that comes from the rear leg of the cow – the round – and which is seasoned with only salt and its fat.

Picanha.

# Chapter 5: Going Sightseeing

« *After a perfect day yesterday, today I think it's time to take a walk around the city and go see its beautiful sights. I just need to know where I have to go. I suppose I could use the GPS... but I have a better idea: I'll hire a tourist guide!* »

"*Bom dia! I was wondering if I can hire your services to guide me along the streets of this city and maybe help me learn a bit of Portuguese along the way, if you wouldn't mind!*"

"*Sure thing, pal! I actually am also a part-time Portuguese teacher, so I'll teach you whatever you want to learn.*"

"*How convenient! This almost seems all conjured up to fit a narrative... Anyway, I've learned quite a bit already. What can you tell me about* **adverbs** **of** **place**, *the*

*conjugation of auxiliary verbs,*
*verb moods and the present*
*form of irregular verbs?"*

*"I can tell you a few things. But let's start by learning how to move around town."*

# 5.1 Around Town

Asking and giving out directions to roam around town is essential if you're visiting a foreign land. Attempting to do it in another language might seem too hard at times, but, in reality, it just takes a bit of practice.

*- Bom dia! Pode dar-me as direcções para o Terreiro do Paço[23], por favor? (Good morning! Can you give me the directions to Terreiro do Paço, please?)*

*- Bom dia! Certamente. É só seguir em frente até ao fim da rua, e depois virar à esquerda. (Good morning! Certainly. You just have to keep going straight ahead up until the end of the street, and then turn left.)*

*- Obrigada! E o elevador de Santa Justa, onde é? (Thank you! And Santa Justa's Elevator, where is it?)*

*- De nada! O elevador fica um pouco mais longe. Tem de atravessar a estrada em direcção ao cruzamento. Quando chegar perto da igreja, vira à*

---

[23] Terreiro do Paço is a famous square by the Tagus river in downtown Lisbon.

---

*direita até ver a rotunda. Na rotunda segue em frente até chegar ao museu. Depois é só virar à esquerda. Também pode apanhar o autocarro - o terminal é já aqui ao virar da esquina. (You're welcome! The elevator is a bit further away. You have to cross the road and head for the crossroads. Once you get to the church, turn right until you see the roundabout. At the roundabout, go straight ahead until you reach the museum. Then you just have to turn left. You can also take the bus - the terminal is right around the corner.)*

*- Eu acho que prefiro ir a pé. E quanto custa o bilhete para subir no elevador? (I think I prefer walking. And how much is the ticket to go up on the elevator?)*

*- Acho que custa 2€. Mas a entrada no museu é grátis. (I think it costs 2€. But the entrance to the museum is free of charge.)*

*- Muito obrigado pela sua ajuda! (Thank you very much for your help!)*

# 5.2 Grammar

### 5.2.1 Adverbs of place

Now, let's talk about adverbs of place. As we learned in the first chapter, adverbs function as an information provider about the verb, adjective, or another adverb, explaining in more detail how the action is occurring. Adverbs of place, in particular, indicate **where** the action is taking place or **where** an object is in space. It answer to the question "ONDE? (Where?)" Take a look at the following examples of adverbs of place:

| Advérbios de lugar | |
|---|---|
| Above | Acima |
| Below | Abaixo |
| Here | Aqui |
| Inside | Dentro |
| Nowhere | Em lado nenhum |
| Over there, beyond | Além |
| Over there, in there | Ali |
| Somewhere | Algures |
| There, then | Aí |

Now, let's watch them in action:

- Os guardanapos estão **além**. (The napkins are over there.)
- **Aqui** não há sobremesas. (There are no desserts here.)
- Ele foi rua **acima**. (He went up the street.)

### 5.2.2 Conjugation of auxiliary verbs

You already know what verbs are, but do you know what auxiliary verbs are? As it happens, verbs can either be main or auxiliary when it comes to their function. If main verbs are tasked with attributing meaning to a sentence, auxiliary verbs are responsible for indicating, for instance, the tense, mode, or voice of the main verbal form. That's why they are also called helping or helper verbs. Take the next two sentences, for example:

"Ele **tem** *estudado* bastante." – "He has been studying a lot."

"A cadeira **foi** *partida* por mim." – "The chair was broken by me."

The verbs in bold are the auxiliary verbs of the main verbs (in italics).

In Portuguese, just like in English, there are quite a few auxiliary verbs, but we are going to focus on the present tense of the most commonly used ones: the verbs "TER," "HAVER," "SER," "ESTAR," "FICAR," and "IR." With the exception of the verb "FICAR," all of the other verbs are irregular, meaning they won't follow the conjugation rules established in chapter 4.

| Verbo TER | |
|---|---|
| Eu | Tenho |
| Tu | Tens |
| Ele/a | Tem |
| Nós | Temos |
| Vós | Tendes |
| Eles/as | Têm |

- Eu **tenho** *comido* muito. (I have been eating a lot.)

- Eles **têm** *saído* à noite ultimamente. (They have been going out at night lately.)

| Verbo HAVER | |
|---|---|
| Eu | Hei |
| Tu | Hás |

| Ele/a | Há |
|-------|-----|
| Nós | Havemos |
| Vós | Haveis |
| Eles/as | Hão |

– Ele **há-de** se *arrepender.* (He will regret it.)
– Nós **havemos** de *conversar.* (We will talk.)

| Verbo SER ||
|-------|-----|
| Eu | Sou |
| Tu | És |
| Ele/a | É |
| Nós | Somos |
| Vós | Sois |
| Eles/as | São |

– Eu **sou** *considerado* culpado. (I am considered guilty.)
– Ela **é** *julgada* amanhã. (She is tried tomorrow.)

| Verbo ESTAR ||
|-------|-----|
| Eu | Estou |
| Tu | Estás |

| Ele/a | Está |
|-------|------|
| Nós | Estamos |
| Vós | Estais |
| Eles/as | Estão |

- Elas **estão** a *falar* dele. (They are speaking about him.)
- Eu **estou** a *andar* devagar. (I am walking slowly.)

## Verbo FICAR

| Eu | Fico |
|-------|------|
| Tu | Ficas |
| Ele/a | Fica |
| Nós | Ficamos |
| Vós | Ficais |
| Eles/as | Ficam |

- Tu **ficas** *vigiando* a casa. (You will stay watching the house.)
- Nós **ficamos** *esperando* aqui. (We will stay waiting here.)

## Verbo IR

| Eu | Vou |
|-------|------|
| Tu | Vais |

| Ele/a | Vai |
|---|---|
| Nós | Vamos |
| Vós | Ides |
| Eles/as | Vão |

– Eles **vão** *sair* agora. (They will leave now.)

– Eu **vou** *convencer-te* eventualmente. (I will convince you eventually.)

### 5.2.3 Verb moods

In Portuguese, just like in English, there are three verbal moods: Indicative, Subjunctive and Imperative. They are used for us to understand how the action is characterized or expressed and what is the speaker's attitude towards it.

In the indicative mood, the verb expresses a certainty, an action that will most likely take place or happen. There are six tenses in the indicative mood: present, perfect indicative, imperfect indicative, pluperfect, future, and conditional.

To understand the differences between them, check out the next tables with the verb "SORRIR (to smile)" conjugated in all of the tenses of these three moods.

| Modo Indicativo | | |
|---|---|---|
| **Presente** | **Pretérito Perfeito** | **Pretérito Imperfeito** |
| Sorrio | Sorri | Sorria |
| Sorris | Sorriste | Sorrias |
| Sorri | Sorriu | Sorria |

| | | |
|---|---|---|
| Sorrimos | Sorrimos | Sorríamos |
| Sorris | Sorristes | Sorrieis |
| Sorriem | Sorriram | Sorriam |

| Modo Indicativo | | |
|---|---|---|
| Mais-que-perfeito | Futuro | Condicional |
| Sorrira | Sorrirei | Sorriria |
| Sorriras | Sorrirás | Sorririas |
| Sorrira | Sorrirá | Sorriria |
| Sorríramos | Sorriremos | Sorriríamos |
| Sorríreis | Sorrireis | Sorriríeis |
| Sorriram | Sorrirão | Sorririam |

The subjunctive mood expresses a non-factual, hypothetical action, expressing the opposite of the indicative mood. There are three tenses in the subjunctive mood: present, imperfect subjunctive, and future tense.

When conjugating a verb in the subjunctive mood, you have to precede the conjugation with the words "QUE (That)" for the present and imperfect tenses and with the words "SE (if)" for the future tense.

| Modo Conjuntivo | | |
|---|---|---|
| **Presente** | **Pretérito Imperfeito** | **Futuro** |
| (Que eu) Sorria | (Que eu) Sorrisse | (Se eu) Sorrir |
| (Que tu) Sorrias | (Que tu) Sorrisses | (Se tu) Sorrires |
| (Que ele / ela) Sorria | (Que ele / ela) Sorrisse | (Se ele / ela) Sorrirem |
| (Que nós) Sorriamos | (Que nós) Sorríssemos | (Se nós) Sorrirmos |
| (Que vós) Sorriais | (Que vós) Sorrísseis | (Se vós) Sorrirdes |
| (Que eles / elas) Sorriam | (Que eles / elas) Sorrissem | (Se eles / elas) Sorrirem |

In the imperative mood, the verb expresses a command, an order, or a request – all depending on the intonation and the context within which it is applied. There are 2 forms of the imperative mood: affirmative and negative.

Something particular about this mood is that there is no conjugation in the first person singular, and if you think about it, it does make sense since you can't command yourself verbally to do something. Also, the subject pronouns are pronounced after the conjugated verb and not before. Like this:

| Modo Imperativo | |
| --- | --- |
| **Afirmativo** | **Negativo** |
| | |
| Sorri (tu) | (não) Sorrias (tu) |
| Sorria (ele / ela) | (não) Sorria (ele / ela) |
| Sorriamos (nós) | (não) Sorriamos (nós) |
| Sorride (vós) | (não) Sorríais (vós) |
| Sorriam (eles / elas) | (não) Sorriam (eles / elas) |

## 5.2.4 Present tense of irregular verbs

In chapter 4, we went through the present tense of regular verbs, which are verbs that keep their stem constant throughout the whole process of conjugation – only the suffix changes. But there are many verbs that are irregular, meaning that their stem changes when conjugated in a non-predictable way. The only way to identify and conjugate irregular verbs is to study and memorize them – there is no other way around it. With that in mind, in the next few pages, you will find the most common irregular verbs in Portuguese in the present tense. Read, study, repeat![24]

---

24 The verbs "TER," "ESTAR," "SER," "HAVER," and "IR" are amongst the most common irregular verbs in the Portuguese language. They were, however, already mentioned and conjugated in a previous sub-chapter (5.2.2), so they will not be repeated in this section.

## Verbo PÔR (to put)

| | |
|---|---|
| Eu | Ponho |
| Tu | Pões |
| Ele/a | Põe |
| Nós | Pomos |
| Vós | Pondes |
| Eles/as | Põem |

## Verbo PODER (to can)

| | |
|---|---|
| Eu | Posso |
| Tu | Podes |
| Ele/a | Pode |
| Nós | Podemos |
| Vós | Podeis |
| Eles/as | Podem |

## Verbo FAZER (to do)

| | |
|---|---|
| Eu | Faço |
| Tu | Fazes |
| Ele/a | Faz |
| Nós | Fazemos |
| Vós | Fazeis |
| Eles/as | Fazem |

## Verbo DAR (to give)

| | |
|---|---|
| Eu | Dou |
| Tu | Dás |
| Ele/a | Dá |
| Nós | Damos |
| Vós | Dais |
| Eles/as | Dão |

## Verbo VIR (to come)

| | |
|---|---|
| Eu | Vou |
| Tu | Vais |
| Ele/a | Vai |
| Nós | Vamos |
| Vós | Vindes |
| Eles/as | Vão |

## Verbo FALAR (to speak)

| | |
|---|---|
| Eu | Falo |
| Tu | Falas |
| Ele/a | Fala |
| Nós | Falamos |
| Vós | Falais |
| Eles/as | Falam |

## Verbo TRAZER (to bring)

| | |
|---|---|
| Eu | Trago |
| Tu | Trazes |
| Ele/a | Traz |
| Nós | Trazemos |
| Vós | Trazeis |
| Eles/as | Trazem |

## Verbo DIZER (to say)

| | |
|---|---|
| Eu | Digo |
| Tu | Dizes |
| Ele/a | Diz |
| Nós | Dizemos |
| Vós | Dizeis |
| Eles/as | Dizem |

## Verbo QUERER (to want)

| | |
|---|---|
| Eu | Quero |
| Tu | Queres |
| Ele/a | Quer |
| Nós | Queremos |
| Vós | Quereis |
| Eles/as | Querem |

## Verbo PEDIR (to ask)

| | |
|---|---|
| Eu | Peço |
| Tu | Pedes |
| Ele/a | Pede |
| Nós | Pedimos |
| Vós | Pedis |
| Eles/as | Pedem |

## Verbo OUVIR (to listen)

| | |
|---|---|
| Eu | Ouço |
| Tu | Ouves |
| Ele/a | Ouve |
| Nós | Ouvimos |
| Vós | Ouvis |
| Eles/as | Ouvem |

## Verbo CABER (to fit)

| | |
|---|---|
| Eu | Caibo |
| Tu | Cabes |
| Ele/a | Cabe |
| Nós | Cabemos |
| Vós | Cabeis |
| Eles/as | Cabem |

# 5.3 Vocabulary

## 5.3.1 Means of transportation

Here's a table with information that is essential in the event of you traveling or even becoming a tour guide:

| English | Portuguese |
|---|---|
| Airplane | Avião |
| Bicycle | Bicicleta |
| Boat | Barco |
| Bus | Autocarro |
| Canoe | Canoa |
| Car | Carro |
| Cruise ship | Navio de Cruzeiro |
| Ferry | Ferry |
| Helicopter | Helicóptero |
| Motorbike | Mota |
| Scooter | Trotinete |
| Ship | Navio |
| Taxi | Táxi |
| Trailer | Atrelado |

| | |
|---|---|
| Train | Comboio |
| Tram | Eléctrico |
| Truck | Camião |
| Underground | Metro |
| Van | Carrinha |

## 5.3.2 Giving directions

The following table is a collection of expressions essential to ask directions to a certain place or to provide them:

| English | Portuguese |
|---|---|
| Close | Perto |
| Crossroads | Cruzamento |
| Far | Longe |
| Go down this street | Descer esta rua |
| Go over | Ir por cima |
| Go under | Ir por baixo |
| Go up this street | Subir esta rua |
| Left | Esquerda |
| Right | Direita |

| | |
|---|---|
| Roundabout | Rotunda |
| Straight ahead | Em frente |
| To continue | Continuar |
| To cross | Atravessar |
| To follow | Seguir |
| To go until | Ir até |
| To turn | Virar |
| On the other side | Do outro lado |

### 5.3.3 Buildings in town

You still have to know the names of the buildings in order to roam around. Here's a list with lots of them:

| English | Portuguese |
|---|---|
| Airport | Aeroporto |
| Bakery | Pastelaria |
| Bank | Banco |
| Book Shop | Livraria |
| Bus station | Terminal de autocarros |
| Bus stop | Paragem de autocarros |

| | |
|---|---|
| Butcher's | Talho |
| Coffee Shop | Café |
| Church | Igreja |
| Clothes' shop | Loja de roupa |
| Dentist | Dentista |
| Fire Station | Quartel de bombeiros |
| Gyn | Ginásio |
| Hairdresser's | Cabeleireiro |
| Hospital | Hospital |
| Museum | Museu |
| Police Station | Esquadra da Polícia |
| Posto Office | Posto dos Correios |
| Restaurant | Restaurante |
| School | Escola |
| Shop | Loja |
| Supermarket | Supermercado |
| Theater | Cinema |

| Train station | Estação de comboios |
|---|---|
| Zoo | Jardim Zoológico |

### 5.3.4 Time expressions for the present

To live in the moment, you need to learn how to speak about the present!

| English | Portuguese |
|---|---|
| In a little while | Daqui a pouco |
| In a minute | Daqui um minuto |
| In an hour | Daqui uma hora |
| In this moment | Neste momento |
| Later | Mais tarde |
| Now | Agora |
| Right now | Já |
| Soon | Logo |
| The time has come | A hora chegou |
| Today | Hoje |
| Tomorrow | Amanhã |

# 5.4 Quiz

You are now halfway into the book, so it's a perfect time for a quiz that encompasses most of the subjects touched on so far. There is something different about this quiz, though: each correct answer is worth 1 point, and out of 61 possible points, you should have a score of at least 30 to pass the quiz. Don't stress about it – it is just a way for you to assess how well you have retained the information provided until now. If you don't pass the test, that is a sign that you would likely be better off revisiting the previous chapters instead of moving on. Good luck!

1) **Turn the following sentences into questions, affirmative or negative statements.**

Eu gosto de chocolate. – _____
(negative statement)

Ele foi à escola. – _____ (question)

Nós não queremos ir ao hospital. – _____
(affirmative statement)

Eles não são Portugueses? _____
(affirmative statement)

Tu pescas todos os dias? – _____
(negative question)

2) **Mark the words that are correctly following the rules of capitalization.**

| | | |
|---|---|---|
| – rio Tejo | – Rua Augusta | – usa |
| – II guerra mundial | – (homem) espanhol | – outono |
| – quarta-feira | – janeiro | – Natal |
| – Dezembro | – Domingo | – john |

3) Complete the blank spaces with the correct form of the verb to be (either "SER" or "ESTAR").

Eu _____ careca. (I am bald.)

_____ frio hoje. (It's cold today.)

Tu _____ alto. (You are tall.)

Nós _____ cansadas. (We are tired.)

Eles _____ casados? (Are they married?)

Ela _____ ali. (She is over there.)

O meu cão _____ castanho. (My dog is brown.)

4) Allocate the words below to their correct place on the table.

| Entre | Demais | Longe |
|-------|--------|-------|
| Algures | Abaixo | Imenso |

| Adverbs of place | Adverbs of quantity | Prepositions of place |
|------------------|---------------------|-----------------------|
|                  |                     |                       |
|                  |                     |                       |

5) Conjugate the following verbs in the present tense: "ESTUDAR," "COMER," "CUMPRIR," and "FAZER."

| Verbo ESTUDAR (to study) | |
|---------|---------|
| Eu |  |
| Tu |  |
| Ele/a |  |

| Nós | |
|---|---|
| Vós | |
| Eles/as | |

## Verbo COMER (to eat)

| Eu | |
|---|---|
| Tu | |
| Ele/a | |
| Nós | |
| Vós | |
| Eles/as | |

## Verbo CUMPRIR (to comply/fulfill)

| Eu | |
|---|---|
| Tu | |
| Ele/a | |
| Nós | |

| | |
|---|---|
| Vós | |
| Eles/as | |

| Verbo FAZER (to do/to make) | |
|---|---|
| Eu | |
| Tu | |
| Ele/a | |
| Nós | |
| Vós | |
| Eles/as | |

6) Identify the mood – indicative, subjunctive, or imperative – in which the following underlined verbs are conjugated.

Come imediatamente! (Eat immediately!)

A minha professora quer que eu estude mais. (My teacher wants me to study more.)

Ele não dorme bem. (He doesn't sleep well.)

Vós sereis os melhores. (You will be the best.)

Tu farias isso por mim? (You would do that for me?)

Eu gostava que tu sorrisses mais. (I would like that you would smile more.)

Não corras por favor! (Don't run please!)

7) With all you have learned so far, write a summary of Tom's journey up until now. It doesn't need to be very structured – just use the vocabulary and grammar you have been studying and use it to write something that sums up what Tom has been up to so far.

# Chapter 6: Having a House Party

« *How kind of that tour guide to invite me to her house party! I'll have to bring my A-game to impress her friends and family with my Portuguese. Well, if they are as nice as she was, I'll ask them about* **direct and indirect object pronouns**, **gender of adjectives**, **possessive adjectives** *and* **possessive pronouns**. *I'm sure that will be useful for longer conversations!* »

"*Boa noite Marta! It's good to be here! Thanks for inviting me.*"

"*Olá Tom! Everyone: this is my American friend Tom. He's here in Lisbon for a vacation and trying to learn Portuguese! Let's all help, shall we?*"

# 6.1 At a party

At any get-together, it is important to get to know each other – especially if you are invited to a house where you don't know the other guests, the small talk that serves as an introduction is perfect for breaking the ice! So, it might be very useful to read the dialogue in which the guests present themselves and explain how they are related to the host.

*"Boa noite a todos! (Goodnight, everybody!)"*

*"Olá, Tom! Bem-vindo à nossa casa. Por favor, fica à vontade e qualquer coisa que precises, é só pedir. (Hello Tom! Welcome to our home. Please, make yourself comfortable, and anything you need, just ask.)"*

*"Obrigadíssimo! (Many thanks!)"*

*"Eu sou a Joana, a mãe da Marta; aquele é o Paulo, pai da Marta; este jovem bonito e forte é o Carlos, o nosso filho mais novo; e aquele rapaz alto e magro é o Filipe, namorado da Marta. (I'm Joana, Marta's mother; that person over there is Paulo, Marta's father; this strong and handsome young man is Carlos, our youngest son; and that tall and thin boy is Filipe, Marta's boyfriend.)"*

*"Prazer em conhecer-vos! Mas antes de entrar em casa, vi uma rapariga perto da porta a falar ao telemóvel. Ela também*

*vem jantar? (Pleasure to meet you all! But before I got in the house, I saw a girl talking on the phone. Is she coming to dinner as well?)"*

*"Como é que ela era? (How did he look like?)"*

*"Bem, ela era baixa, tinha cabelo comprido, loiro; uns grandes olhos castanhos e um nariz muito delicado. (Well, she was short, had a long blonde hair; big brown eyes and very delicate nose.)"*

*"Ah, deve ser a Sara, a nossa vizinha. Não, ela não vem jantar. Mas a Mariana, a melhor amiga da Marta, vem! Ela é uma miúda alta, atlética com o cabelo sempre em trança. É linda – de certeza que vais gostar dela. (Ha, it must be Sara, our neighbour. No, she is not coming to dinner. But Mariana, Marta's best friend, is coming! She is a tall athletic girl, always with a French braid. She is beautiful – surely you will like her.)"*

# 6.2 Grammar

## 6.2.1 Direct & indirect object pronouns

So, regarding direct and indirect object pronouns, the first thing you should know is that they each answer different questions. What that means is that to substitute the noun for the correct pronoun, you need to ask a question that is prompted by the sentence itself. Confused? Well, it will all become clear in no time.

As you know, sentences sometimes have objects. That is true when there is a transitive verb that demands an object, meaning that the sentence won't make sense if the sentence just has the verb by itself. Case in point:

- Eu chamo. (I call.)

or

- Ele emprestou. (He lent.)

You probably found yourself immediately asking – "I call **whom?**" and "He lent **what?**" Well, for these sentences to make sense, they have to have an object; the transitive verbs "CHAMAR (to call)" and "EMPRESTAR (to lend)" demand it. So, continuing the example:

- Eu chamo *o Diogo.* (I call Diogo.)

- Ele emprestou *a bicicleta.* (He lent the bike.)

Now, the questions that were asked before are answered – the answers "O DIOGO" and "A BICICLETA (the bike)" are the direct objects.

The following are the **direct object pronouns**:

| Direct object pronouns | Pronomes de complemento directo |
|---|---|
| Me | Me |
| You | Te |
| Him / Her / It | O / A |
| Us | Nos |
| You | Vos |
| Them | Os / As |

As stated above, the direct object can be identified by asking the questions "O QUÊ? (what?)," or "QUEM? (who/whom?)" So, those are the nouns that direct object pronouns are going to substitute. Like this:

– Eu chamo **o Diogo**. (I call Diogo.) – Eu chamo-**o**. (I call him.)

– Ele emprestou **a bicicleta**. (He lent the bike.) – Ele emprestou-**a**. (He lent it.)

As for the indirect object, you can identify it within a sentence by asking the questions "A QUEM? (to whom?)," "PARA QUEM? (for whom?)," and "DE QUEM? (from whom?)." For instance:

– Ela contou um segredo ao José. (She told José a secret.) – Ela contou um segredo **a quem**? *Ao José*. (She told a secret to whom? To José.)

– Nós comemos o bolo das cozinheiras. (We ate the cook's cake.) – Nós comemos o bolo **de quem**? *Das cozinheiras*. (We ate whose cake? The cook's.)

The following are the **indirect object pronouns**:

| Indirect object pronouns | Pronomes de complemento indirecto |
|---|---|
| Me | Me |
| You | Te |
| Him / Her / It | Lhe |
| Us | Nos |
| You | Vos |
| Them | Lhes |

Now, in order to use the pronouns displayed in the previous table, we just need to switch the already identified indirect objects for the correct pronouns.

- Ela contou um segredo **ao José**. (She told José a secret.) – Ela contou-*lhe* um segredo. (She told him a secret.)

- Nós comemos o bolo **das cozinheiras**. (We ate the cooks' cake.) – Nós comemos-*lhes* o bolo. (We ate their cake.)

## Location of the pronoun

What might seem confusing now is the location of the pronouns within the sentence. So, what you will have to memorize – and this applies to both direct and indirect object pronouns – is that the rule is **the pronoun goes after the verb** and is separated by a hyphen. This is the most common situation – nevertheless, as always, there are exceptions.

Let's go through the five exceptional situations in which the pronoun must be placed *before* the verb:

1) When there is an **adverb**:

- Ele <u>apenas</u> emprestou a bicicleta. (He only lent the bike.) – Ele apenas *a* emprestou. (He only lent it.)

- Eu <u>também</u> contei um segredo ao José. (I also told José a secret.) – Eu também *lhe* contei um segredo. (I also told him a secret.)

2) When it is a **negative** statement:

- Ele <u>não</u> emprestou a bicicleta. (He didn't lend his bike). – Ele não *a* emprestou. (He didn't lend it.)

- Eu <u>não</u> contei um segredo ao José. (I didn't tell José a secret.) – Eu não *lhe* contei um segredo. (I didn't tell him a secret.)

3) When it is a **question**:

- <u>Quem</u> emprestou a bicicleta? (Who lent the bike?) – Quem *a* emprestou? (Who lent it?)

- <u>Quem</u> contou um segredo ao José? (Who told José a secret?) – Quem *lhe* contou um segredo? (Who told him a secret?)

4) When there are **relative pronouns**:

- Ele disse <u>que</u> emprestou a bicicleta. (He said that he lent the bike.) – Ele disse que *a* emprestou. (He said that he lent it.)

- Eu acho <u>que</u> contei um segredo ao José. (I think I told José a secret.) – Eu acho que *lhe* contei um segredo. (I think I told him a secret.)

    5) When there are **prepositions**:

    - Ele está triste <u>desde</u> que emprestou a bicicleta. (He is sad since he lent the bike.) – Ele está triste desde que **<u>a</u>** emprestou. (He is sad since he lent it.)

    - Eles disseram-me <u>para</u> contar um segredo ao José. (They told me to tell José a secret.) – Eles disseram-me para **_lhe_** contar um segredo. (They told me to tell him a secret.)

## Verbs ending with the letters "S," "R," or "Z"

Another important thing to mention is that when verbs end with the letters mentioned above, the last letters of the verb should be dropped, and an "L" should be added to the beginning of the pronouns "O," "A," "OS" or "AS." For instance:

    - Tu quere<u>s</u> chocolate. (You want chocolate.) – Tu quere-**<u>lo</u>**. (You want it.)

    - Eles estão a come<u>r</u> peixe. (They are eating fish.) – Eles estão a comê-**<u>lo</u>**. (They are eating it.)

    - Ela fa<u>z</u> bolos. (She makes cakes.) – Ela fá-**<u>los</u>**. (She makes them.)

# Verbs ending with a nasal sound

When it comes to verbs ending with the nasal sound "M," you should keep the verb as it is and add an "N" to the pronoun. This happens just so it is easier to pronounce the verb with the pronoun that follows. For instance:

    - Elas bebem café. (They drink coffee.) – Elas bebem-**_<u>no</u>_**. (They drink it.)

    - Eles roubaram a senhora. (They robbed the lady.) – Eles roubaram-**_<u>na</u>_**. (They robbed her.)

## Sentences with direct and indirect objects

It's true that there can either be sentences with only a direct object and sentences with only an indirect object, but what if there are direct and indirect objects in the same sentence? For instance, some of the example sentences we have been working with have both objects – how do we use the pronouns then?

In this first sentence, we have both direct and indirect objects but notice that only the **direct object** is substituted:

- Eu contei **um segredo** ao José. (I told José a secret.) Eu contei-**o** ao José. (I told it to José).

In this one, only the **indirect object** is substituted:

- Eu contei um segredo **ao José**. (I told José a secret.) Eu contei-**lhe** um segredo. (I told him a secret.)

But if we wanted to substitute both, we could. To do that, the pronouns must contract. Like this:

- Eu contei um segredo ao José. (I told José a secret.) Eu contei-**_lho_**. (I told it to him.)

- Ele emprestou a bicicleta à Maria. (He lent the bike to Maria.) Ele emprestou-**_lha_**. (He lent it to her.)

Notice that in the first sentence, the direct object pronoun "O" merged with the indirect object pronoun "LHE." In the second one, the indirect object pronoun "LHE" also merged, but this time with the direct object pronoun "A" since the word "BICICLETA (bike)" is feminine. Check out a few more examples for you to get the hang of it:

- Ela ofereceu um presente a mim. (She offered a gift to me.) – Ela ofereceu-**_mo_**. (She offered it to me.) ME + O = MO

- Eu dei um cachecol a ti. (I gave a scarf to you.) – Eu dei-**_to_**. (I gave it to you.) TE + O = TO

- Tu partiste as janelas da Catarina e do Bruno. (You broke Catarina's and Bruno's windows.) – Tu partiste-**_lhas_**. (You broke their windows.) LHES + AS = LHAS.

### 6.2.2 Gender of adjectives

In Portuguese, just like determiners, adjectives must also agree in gender with the word they are describing. Therefore, you must first identify the gender of the noun (either by checking the ending of the word or by the determinant that precedes the noun), so you can use the adjective in the correct gender.

Luckily, many of the rules that apply to the gender of nouns also apply to the gender of adjectives. That's the case because many nouns can turn into adjectives and vice-versa.

So, let's recapitulate the rules about the gender of nouns that adjectives share.

# Adjectives ending in "ÃO"

To change the masculine gender of adjectives that end with the diphthong "ÃO," the most common suffix modifications are:

- The "O" drops;
- The "ÃO" turns into "ONA."

| English | Masculine | Feminine |
|---|---|---|
| Healthy | S**ão** | S**ã** |
| Orphan | Orf**ão** | Orf**ã** |
| "Cry baby" | Chor**ão** | Chor**ona** |
| Swashbuckler | Fanfarr**ão** | Fanfarr**ona** |

# Adjectives ending in "OR," "ÊS," and "U"

With adjectives with these three endings, a simple "A" needs to be added.

| English | Masculine | Feminine |
|---|---|---|
| Charming | Encantad**or** | Encantad**ora** |
| Conservative | Conservad**or** | Conservad**ora** |
| French | Franc**ês** | Franc**esa** |
| English | Ingl**ês** | Ingl**esa** |

| | | |
|---|---|---|
| Raw | Cr<u>u</u> | Cr<u>ua</u> |
| Naked | N<u>u</u> | N<u>ua</u> |

# Adjectives ending in "EU"

Lastly, when adjectives end in "EU," we usually just need to swap those letters for the letters "EIA." Like this:

| English | Masculine | Feminine |
|---|---|---|
| Commoner | Pleb<u>eu</u> | Pleb<u>eia</u> |
| Hebrew | Hebr<u>eu</u> | Hebr<u>eia</u> |

### 6.2.3 Possessive adjectives

Possessive adjectives (or "determinantes possessivos" in Portuguese) are a class of words that precedes the noun in a sentence, determining to whom that noun belongs. The following table lists all the possessive adjectives there are:

| DETERMINANTES POSSESSIVOS | | |
|---|---|---|
| English | Singular | Plural |
| My | Meu / Minha | Meus / Minhas |
| Your | Teu / Tua | Teus / Tuas |
| His / Hers / Its | Seu / Sua | Seus / Suas |
| Our | Nosso / Nossa | Nossos / Nossas |
| Your | Vosso / Vossa | Vossos / Vossas |
| Their | Seu / Sua | Seus / Suas |

Check out the next few phrases:

- Esta é a **minha** casa. (This is my house.)
- Aquele é o **teu** casaco? (Is that your jacket?)
- O **meu** irmão é gordo. (My brother is fat.)
- As **nossas** cadeiras partiram-se. (Our chairs broke.)

The word "MINHA" in the first sentence indicates to whom the house belongs. The word "TEU" in the second sentence indicates to whom the jacket belongs[25]. The word "MEU" in the third sentence indicates whose brother it is, and finally, the word "NOSSAS" in the last sentence indicates to whom the chairs belong.

### 6.2.4 Possessive pronouns

While pronouns substitute nouns, possessive pronouns do that while indicating possession. Just like possessive adjectives, they add information about to whom something belongs. What might be tricky about differentiating these two classes of words is that they are actually the same in Portuguese. On the other hand, in English, there are different terms for both classes of words, even though they are very similar to each other, so in the next table, you will see the English terms correspond to the exact same words you saw in the previous sub-chapter:

| PRONOMES POSSESSIVOS | | |
|---|---|---|
| **English** | **Singular** | **Plural** |
| Mine | Meu / Minha | Meus / Minhas |
| Yours | Teu / Tua | Teus / Tuas |
| His / Hers | Seu / Sua | Seus / Suas |

---

25 Technically, as it is a question, it asks (directly) to whom the jacket belongs, while insinuating that it belongs to "YOU (your jacket)."

---

| Ours | Nosso / Nossa | Nossos / Nossas |
| Yours | Vosso / Vossa | Vossos / Vossas |
| Theirs | Seu / Sua | Seus / Suas |

But what changes then? Well, since they are pronouns, they indicate possession **and** substitute the noun. They answer the question "DE QUEM?" (whose?)

Taking the same sentences from the previous sub-chapter:

– "Esta é a minha casa." (This is my house.) "Casa de quem? **Minha**." (Whose house? Mine.)

– "Aquele é o teu casaco?" (Is that your jacket?) "Casaco de quem? **Teu**." (Whose jacket? Yours.)

– "O meu irmão é gordo." (My brother is fat.) "O **teu** não é." (Yours isn't.)

– "As nossas cadeiras partiram-se." (Our chairs broke.) "As **vossas** estão boas?" (Are yours ok?)

Notice that in these cases, the underlined words substitute the noun. If you were to answer with the noun following the word, then it would be a possessive adjective – not a possessive pronoun.

# 6.3 Vocabulary

## 6.3.1 Family members

To impress your close ones at the next holiday reunion, check out this table to know how to name all of the family members in Portuguese:

| **English** | **Portuguese** |
| --- | --- |
| Aunt | Tia |
| Best friend | Melhor amigo |

| | |
|---|---|
| Boyfriend | Namorado |
| Brother | Irmão |
| Brother-in-law | Cunhado |
| Cousin | Primo |
| Daughter | Filha |
| Daughter-in-law | Nora |
| Family | Família |
| Father-in-law | Sogro |
| Fiancé | Noivo |
| Friend | Amigo |
| Girlfriend | Namorada |
| Goddaughter | Afilhada |
| Godfather | Padrinho |
| Godmother | Madrinha |
| Godson | Afilhado |
| Granddaughter | Neta |
| Grandfather | Avô |

| | |
|---|---|
| Grandmother | Avó |
| Grandparents | Avós |
| Grandson | Neto |
| Husband | Marido |
| Mother-in-law | Sogra |
| Nephew | Sobrinho |
| Niece | Sobrinha |
| Sister | Irmã |
| Sister-in-law | Cunhada |
| Son | Filho |
| Son-in-law | Genro |
| Stepdaughter | Enteada |
| Stepfather | Padrasto |
| Stepmother | Madrasta |
| Stepson | Enteado |
| Uncle | Tio |
| Wife | Esposa |

### 6.3.2 The Human Body

The following list is not for you to impress a Portuguese doctor as much as it is for the doctor to know what is wrong with you. It might be important in an urgent situation in which the doctor isn't as multilingual as you are!

| English | Portuguese |
|---|---|
| Ankle | Tornozelo |
| Arm | Braço |
| Armpit | Axila/Sovaco |
| Back | Costas |
| Backbone | Coluna vertebral |
| Beard | Barba |
| Belly | Barriga |
| Belly button | Umbigo |
| Big toe | Dedo grande |
| Bladder | Bexiga |
| Blood | Sangue |
| Bone | Osso |
| Bottom | Rabo |
| Brain | Cérebro |

| | |
|---|---|
| Breasts | Seios |
| Calf (body part) | Gémeo |
| Cheek | Bochecha |
| Chest | Peito |
| Chin | Queixo |
| Ear | Orelha/Ouvido[26] |
| Elbow | Cotovelo |
| Eye | Olho |
| Eyebrow | Sobrancelha |
| Eyelash | Pestana |
| Finger | Dedo |
| Foot | Pé |
| Forehead | Testa |
| Fur | Pêlo |
| Hair | Cabelo |

[26] Even though in English there is just one term to refer to the ear, in Portuguese, "orelha" is used when talking about the outer part of the ear, while "ouvido" is used when talking about the inner part of the ear.

| | |
|---|---|
| Hand | Mão |
| Head | Cabeça |
| Heart | Coração |
| Heel | Calcanhar |
| Hip | Anca |
| Intestines | Intestinos |
| Jaw | Maxilar |
| Kidneys | Rins |
| Knee | Joelho |
| Kneecap | Rótula |
| Leg | Perna |
| Lip | Lábio |
| Liver | Fígado |
| Lungs | Pulmões |
| Mouth | Boca |
| Muscle | Músculo |
| Mustache | Bigode |

| | |
|---|---|
| Neck | Pescoço |
| Nose | Nariz |
| Nostril | Narina |
| Rib | Costela |
| Shoulder | Ombro |
| Skin | Pele |
| Skull | Crânio |
| Stomach | Estômago |
| Teeth | Dentes |
| Thigh | Coxa |
| Throat | Garganta |
| Thumb | Polegar |
| Toe | Dedo do pé |
| Tongue | Língua |
| Tooth | Dente |
| Urine | Urina |
| Vein | Veia |

| | |
|---|---|
| Vertebra | Vértebra |
| Waist | Cintura |
| Wrist | Pulso |

### 6.3.3 Describing people' appearance

In the following table, you will find a list of adjectives to help you describe yourself and others. To make it easier for you to navigate through and find what you need, you will find an adjective and its antonym (the adjective with the opposite meaning) right after it.

| **English** | **Portuguese** |
|---|---|
| Bald ≠ Hairy | Careca ≠ Cabeludo/a |
| Beautiful ≠ Ugly | Bonito/a ≠ Feio/a |
| Dark skin ≠ light skin | Pele escura ≠ Pele clara |
| Gorgeous ≠ Hideous | Lindo/a ≠ Horrendo/a |
| Muscular ≠ Slim | Musculado/a ≠ Esguio/a |
| Short hair ≠ long hair | Cabelo curto ≠ Cabelo comprido |
| Tall ≠ Short | Alto/a ≠ Baixo/a |
| Tanned ≠ Pale | Bronzeado/a ≠ Pálido/a |
| Thin ≠ Fat | Magro/a ≠ Gordo/a |
| Young ≠ Old | Novo/a ≠ Velho/a |

# 6.4 Home-visiting etiquette

Since this chapter was dedicated to going to a house party, it might be very useful to add some tips on what to offer when visiting somebody's home. Before we start, it might be useful to add that both Portugal and Brazil have very similar home-visiting etiquette, so you really will be fine taking the advice that follows in any of these two countries.

Firstly, what is most likely the biggest difference you will notice between a country like the United States and Portugal or Brazil (or any Latin country for that matter), is that people are very warm and touching, which is by no means intended as flirting. When greeting someone – except in a business or professional situation – the norm is to give two kisses on each cheek. This only does not apply to men greeting men – they usually just give each other a handshake. When you are talking to somebody informally, expect a lot of hand gestures and slight touches on the arms and hands.

Secondly, when visiting somebody's home, especially if you've been invited for a meal, it is recommended that you bring something. If you are going to have lunch or dinner, a wine bottle is fine – even though you should ask beforehand if you should bring red or white. Chocolate boxes, whiskey, a dessert, or flowers (for the hostess) are also appropriate.

If there was a set time in your invitation, being up to 15 minutes late is probably okay, since more often than not, Portuguese and Brazilians tend to lack in punctuality! If you're going to be more than 15 minutes late, you should probably call ahead to let your hosts know about it.

When entering somebody's home, you should let the host guide you along the house and only sit when invited to. Also, keep in mind that if somebody offers you a gift, it is common practice to open it in front of the person who gave it to you.

After visiting somebody's home, good manners suggest that you should also invite your hosts back for some event in the future.

# Chapter 7: Eating Out

«*What a nice dinner we had! I feel like I'm ready to go out and venture the city on my own. Tomorrow I'll have lunch at a restaurant and try to speak with the waiter only in Portuguese. But since I have some time up until then, there are some things I'd like to go through first, in order to be more prepared. Let's see what my language learning app has for its lesson of the day...* **Comparatives and superlatives of adjectives, adverbs of mode**, *and* **conjunctions**? *Cool!* »*

## 7.1 At a restaurant

At a restaurant, the most important things for you to know is how to ask for the menu, food, and drinks in a clear and polite way. However, when visiting a foreign country, there probably will be many dishes with which you are not familiar. Hence, you will need to ask for descriptions of dishes on the menu, compare them with each other and finally make a choice. This next dialogue will demonstrate exactly that situation. After it, you will surely be able to talk for hours about your favorite food!

"Boa noite. Tem mesa para uma pessoa, por favor? (Good evening. Do you have a table for one person, please?)"

"Certamente. Quer mesa de fumadores ou de não-fumadores? (Certainly. Do you want a table for smokers or non-smokers?)"

"De não-fumadores, por favor. (For non-smokers, please.)"

"Muito bem. Por favor, acompanhe-me. Esta é a sua mesa. Aqui está o menu. O que vai querer para beber? (Very well, please follow me. This is your table. Here is the menu. What will you want to drink?)"

"Uma caneca de vinho verde da casa, por favor. E uma garrafa de água, fresca. (A jug of house vinho verde[27], please. And a bottle of water, cooled.)"

"E para comer? (And to eat?)"

"O que recomenda? (What do you recommend?)"

---

27 Literally, it translates to green wine, but it's meant to have the meaning of green as in young. It's a famous Portuguese, slightly sparkling, wine that is released for consumption three to six months after the grapes are harvested!

---

"O prato do dia é o bitoque com ovo a cavalo e molho de café, acompanhado de batatas fritas e salada. O bitoque é um bife de vitela, com um ovo estrelado por cima. (The dish of the day is the "bitoque com ovo a cavalo" in a coffee sauce, accompanied by French fries and a salad. The "bitoque" is a veal beef with a fried egg on top.)"

"Parece delicioso. E que pratos de peixe têm? (Sounds delicious. And what fish dishes do you have?)"

"Temos uma excelente açorda de camarão e cataplana à Algarvia. A açorda é um saboroso prato que consiste em pão embebido em azeite, alho, ervas aromáticas, ovos e camarão. A cataplana é um prato típico do Algarve (sul de Portugal), à base de tamboril, amêijoas, alho e presunto. (We have an excelente shrimp "açorda" and an algarvian "cataplana." The "açorda" is a tasty dish that consists of bread soaked in olive oil, garlic, aromatic herbs, eggs, and shrimp. The "cataplana" is a typical dish from Algarve (south of Portugal), with a monkfish, clams, garlic, and ham base.)"

"A cataplana convenceu-me! Traga-me meia-dose, por favor. (The "cataplana" convinced me! Bring me a half portion, please.)"

"Obrigado. Pode só dizer-me onde fica a casa de banho, por favor? (Thank you. Can you just tell me where the bathroom is, please?)"

... [A few minutes later...]

"Obrigado! (Thank you!)"

"Está tudo fantástico. (Everything is fantastic.)"

[Some more minutes later...]

"Desculpe! Pode trazer-me um café[28] e uma água com

"Muito bem! (Very well!)"

"É ao fundo daquele corredor à direita. (Is at the of that hall to the right.)"

"Aqui está a sua comida. Bom apetite! (Here is your food. Enjoy!)"

[Some time later...]

"Está tudo bem por aqui? Está a gostar da sua refeição? (Is everything good around here? Are you enjoying your meal?)"

---

28 In Portugal, if you ask for just a "café (coffee)," everyone will serve you an expresso. So, if you want to order something different, for instance an American type of coffee, you will

gás, se não se importa? (Excuse me! Can you bring me an expresso and a sparkling water, if you don't mind?)"

"É para já. Aceita um digestivo? Talvez um vinho do Porto? É um vinho típico português, fortificado e doce, perfeito para o fim da refeição. (I will do that right away. Will you accept a digestive? Perhaps a Port wine? It's a typical Portuguese wine, fortified and sweet, perfect for after the meal.)"

"Parece-me óptimo! Já agora, traga-me também a conta, por favor. (That sounds great! While we are at it, bring me the check as well, please.)"

"Vai pagar em dinheiro ou cartão de crédito? (Will you pay in cash or credit-card)?"

"Em dinheiro. (In cash.)"

"Aqui está. Esperamos que tenha gostado da sua refeição. (Here it is. We hope you like your meal.)"

---

have to explain that in your order.

---

# 7.2 Grammar

## 7.2.1 Comparatives and superlatives of adjectives

As you know, adjectives are used to attribute traits or characteristics to nouns. They give the interlocutor more information about the person, animal, or thing that is being talked about. But just like in English, adjectives have degrees. The positive (or normal) degree, the comparative, and the superlative. The positive degree adjectives just characterize something with no indication of its intensity or its relationship to something else. For instance:

- A minha casa é **bonita**. (My house is beautiful.)
- Eu sou **alto**. (I am tall.)
- Eles são **importantes.** (They are important.)

# Comparative degree

Comparative adjectives, on the other hand, compare the same characteristic between two or more things. For example:

- A minha casa é **menos bonita que** a tua. (My house is less beautiful than yours.)
- Eu sou **tão alto quanto** ele. (I am as tall as him.)
- Eles são **mais importantes do que** vocês. (They are more important than you.)

Perhaps you noticed that the comparisons establish different relationships; that is because, within the comparative degree, there are three sub-degrees: inferiority, equality, and superiority degree.

In the *inferiority comparative* degree, a relationship of inferiority is established using the words "MENOS QUE" (less than).

In the *equality comparative* degree, a relationship of equality is established using the words "TÃO" (as), and "COMO / QUANTO / QUÃO" (as).

In the *superiority comparative* degree, a relationship of superiority is established using the words "MAIS QUE" (more than).

Let's take a look at a few more examples:

| Normal / positive | Inferiority comparative degree | Equality comparative degree | Superiority comparative degree |
|---|---|---|---|
| Baixo (short) | Menos baixo que | Tão baixo quanto | Mais baixo que |
| Inteligente (intelligent) | Menos inteligente que | Tão inteligente quanto | Mais inteligente que |
| Bonita (beautiful) | Menos bonita que | Tão bonita como | Mais bonita que |

However, this doesn't apply to all adjectives since there are a few that form the superiority comparative degree in an irregular way:

| Normal / positive | Superiority comparative |
|---|---|
| Bom (good) | Melhor (better) |
| Mau (bad) | Pior (worse) |
| Grande (big) | Maior (bigger) |
| Pequeno (small) | Menor (smaller) |

# Superlative degree

When it comes to superlative adjectives, they don't compare one thing to another; they instead establish a relationship between a thing (or several) and other things. They also sub-divide into relative and absolute superlatives.

Regarding the **relative superlative** degree, there can either be relative superlative of inferiority adjectives or relative superlative of superiority adjectives. For instance:

- A minha casa é **a mais bonita**. (My house is the most beautiful.)
- Eu sou **o mais alto**. (I am the tallest.)
- Eles são **os mais importantes.** (They are the most important ones.)

The previous sentences were all using the relative superlative of superiority. That relationship is established using the words "O / A MAIS" (the most). The relative superlative of inferiority is established using the words "O / A MENOS" (the least). Like this:

- A minha casa é **a menos bonita**. (My house is the least beautiful.)
- Eu sou **o menos alto**. (I am the least tall.)
- Eles são **os menos importantes.** (They are the least important ones.)

Regarding the **absolute superlative** degree, it characterizes a thing or more while intensifying the adjective. There can be either analytical absolute superlative adjectives or synthetic absolute superlative adjectives. While the a) first sub-group is formed by simply adding an intensifying adverb that precedes the adjective (very commonly "MUITO (very)," the b) second sub-group takes on a more concise form, adding a suffix to the adjective, and thus forming a new word.

a)  – A minha casa é **muito bonita**. (My house is very beautiful.)

b)  – A minha casa é **bonitíssima**. (My house is gorgeous.)

a)  – Eu sou **extremamente alto**. (I am extremely tall.)

b)  – Eu sou **altíssimo**. (I am enormous.)

a)  – Eles são **imensamente importantes.** (They are immensely important.)

b)  – Eles são **importantíssimos.** (They are paramount.)

Now a few notes as to how the synthetic absolute superlative is formed. The suffix can adopt one of these options "-ÍSSIMO," "-ÍLIMO," and "-ÉRRIMO." Unfortunately, there are no rules to follow, so you will just have to memorize how the synthetic absolute superlatives of adjectives look. Here is a table from which you can study some of them:

| Normal / positive | Synthetic absolute superlative |
|---|---|
| Amigo (friendly) | Amicíssimo |
| Difícil (hard) | Dificílimo |
| Doce (sweet) | Dulcíssimo / docíssimo |
| Fácil (easy) | Facílimo |
| Feio (ugly) | Feiíssimo |
| Feliz (happy) | Felicíssimo |
| Horrível (horrible) | Horribilíssimo |
| Pobre (poor) | Paupérrimo |
| Rico (rich) | Riquíssimo |
| Simpático (nice) | Simpaticíssimo |
| Triste (triste) | Tristíssimo |

Lastly, there are some exceptions. Those adjectives that formed an irregular superiority comparative also form irregular superlatives:

| Normal / positive | Superiority comparative | Relative superlative of superiority | Synthetic absolute superlative |
|---|---|---|---|
| Bom (good) | Melhor (better) | O melhor (the best) | Óptimo (great) |
| Mau (bad) | Pior (worse) | O pior (the worst) | Péssimo (awful) |
| Grande (big) | Maior (bigger) | O maior (the biggest) | Enorme (enormous) |
| Pequeno (small) | Menor (smaller) | O menor (the smallest) | Mínimo (minimal) |

### 7.2.2 Adverbs of mode

Now, let's talk about adverbs of mode. As you're tired of knowing by now, adverbs function as an information provider about the verb, adjective, or another adverb. Adverbs of mode, in particular, indicate *how* the action is taking place. It answers the question, "Como? (How)" Take a look at the following examples of adverbs of mode:

| Advérbios de modo | |
|---|---|
| Badly | Mal |
| Carefully | Cuidadosamente |
| Easily | Facilmente |

| Quickly | Rapidamente |
|---------|-------------|
| Slowly | Devagar |
| Slowly | Lentamente |
| Thus, therefore | Assim |
| Well, right | Bem |

### 7.2.3 Conjunctions[29]

As was stated in the first chapter, conjunctions are bridges between the elements of a sentence. However, these two parts of the sentence are not always dependent on each other to make sense, *i.e.,* they sometimes can be in an independent phrase and still make sense. There can either be **coordinating** or **subordinating** conjunctions.

*Coordinating conjunctions* establish a relationship between two coordinated clauses of the same nature. They connect independent clauses and are divided into:

### 1) Additive

Additive conjunctions establish a relationship of addition – of summation. For example:

– Ele **não só** estuda, **como também** trabalha. (He not only studies but also works.)

– Já fiz exercício **e** agora vou descansar. (I already exercised, and now I am going to sleep.)

---

29 The translations of the Portuguese conjunctions to the English language are only an approximation since it would only be possible to translate them properly in a specific sentence.

---

| English | Portuguese |
|---|---|
| And | E |
| Nor | Nem |
| Not only... but also | Não só... mas /como também |
| Both... and | Tanto... como |
| Neither... nor | Nem... nem |

## 2) Adversarial

Adversarial conjunctions establish a relationship of opposition or contrast. For example:

– O Carlos queria ir ao cinema, **contudo** não tinha dinheiro. (Carlos wanted to go to the movies; he didn't have money, however.)

– Ela dormiu muito; **ainda assim**, tinha sono. (She slept a lot; still, she was sleepy.)

| English | Portuguese |
|---|---|
| But | Mas |
| However | Contudo |
| Nevertheless | Todavia |
| Yet | Porém |
| Albeit | Não obstante |

| Though | Apesar disso |
|---|---|
| Still | Ainda assim |
| Nonetheless | No entanto |

### 3) Alternative

Alternative conjunctions establish a relationship of choice of thoughts, disjunction or alternative. For instance:

– Ela **ora** corria, **ora** parava. (She would run, and stop, and run and stop.)

– **Ou** páras **ou** eu chateio-me. (Either you stop or I'll get angry.)

| **English** | **Portuguese** |
|---|---|
| Or | Ou |
| Either... or | Ou... ou |
| Whether | Quer... quer |
| Be it... be it | Seja... seja |
| Either... or | Ora... ora |

### 4) Conclusive

Conclusive conjunctions establish a relationship of the conclusion of thought since they connect two clauses, one being the conclusion of the other. For example:

– O frango saiu do forno, **portanto** está quente. (The chicken came out of the oven; therefore, it is hot.)

– Estou habituado, **por isso** não tenho frio. (I'm used to it, so I'm not cold.)

| English | Portuguese |
|---|---|
| Since | Pois |
| Therefore | Portanto |
| Thus | Logo |
| So | Assim |
| Ergo | Por conseguinte |
| Consequently | Por consequência |
| So | Por isso |

## 5) Explicative

Explicative conjunctions establish a relationship of explanation – that includes reason and motive. For instance:

- Eu festejei, **porquanto** era o meu dia de aniversário. (I celebrated since it was my birthday.)

- Ela chorou, **pois** estava triste. (She cried, for she was sad.)

| English | Portuguese |
|---|---|
| Since | Pois |
| As | Porque |
| That | Que |
| Since | Porquanto |

*Subordinating conjunctions* establish a relationship of dependence between two clauses, in which one is the main clause, and the other is the subordinate. They are divided into:

1) **Causal**

Causal conjunctions introduce a subordinate clause that gives an indication of motive. For instance:

- Eu chumbei, **porque** não estudei. (I flunked because I didn't study.)

- **Como** está a chover, preciso de um guarda-chuva. (As it is raining, I need an umbrella.)

| English | Portuguese |
|---------|------------|
| Because | Porque |
| As | Como |
| Since | Porquanto |

2) **Temporal**

Temporal conjunctions establish a temporal relationship. For instance:

- Eu vou à praia **sempre que** posso. (I go to the beach whenever I can.)

- **Quando** chegares lá, avisa. (When you get there, let me know.)

| English | Portuguese |
|---------|------------|
| When | Quando |
| While | Enquanto |
| Only | Apenas |

| | |
|---|---|
| As soon as | Logo que |
| After than | Depois que |
| Before than | Antes que |
| Until | Até que |
| Whenever | Sempre que |
| Whenever | Todas as vezes que |
| Now that | Agora que |
| Each time | Cada vez que |
| Once that | Assim que |
| Insofar as | À medida que |

### 3) Final

Final conjunctions indicate a finality, an objective, a purpose. For instance:

- **De modo a que** não fique preso no trânsito, eu vou sair mais cedo de casa. (In order not to get stuck in traffic, I will leave the house earlier.)

- Ele come pouco **para** não engordar. (He eats little so that he won't get fat.)

| English | Portuguese |
|---|---|
| So that | Para |
| In order to | Para que |

| | |
|---|---|
| In order to | De modo a que |
| However | Por... que |
| In order to | A fim de |
| So that | De forma a que |

### 4) Conditional

Conditional conjunctions introduce a condition or a hypothesis. For instance:

- Estarei disponível, **caso** mudes de ideias. (I will be available in case you change your mind.)

- Eles não vão, **a não ser que** tu venhas também. (They won't come unless you come as well.)

| English | Portuguese |
|---|---|
| If | Se |
| Supposing | Caso |
| Provided that | Desde que |
| Unless | Salvo se |
| Except if | Excepto se |
| Unless | A menos que |
| Unless | A não ser que |
| As long as | Contanto que |

## 5) Concessive

Concessive conjunctions establish a relationship of objection, of difficulty. For instance:

- **Ainda que** tivesse fome, o Ricardo não queria comer sopa. (In spite of being hungry, Ricardo didn't want to eat soup.)

- Ela gosta de jogar ténis, **embora** não goste de assistir. (She likes playing tennis, even though she doesn't like watching it.)

| English | Portuguese |
|---|---|
| Even though | Embora |
| Notwithstanding | Conquanto |
| Albeit | Se bem que |
| Despite | Malgrado |
| Though | Posto que |
| Even if | Ainda que |
| Even though | Mesmo que |
| In spite of | Apesar de |

## 6) Consecutive

Consecutive conjunctions introduce an idea of the consequence of what was previously declared. For instance:

- Havia muito trânsito, **de modo que** se atrasou. (There was a lot of traffic, so she was late.)

- Eu não tenho dinheiro, **de maneira que** não vou comprar nada. (I don't have money, so I won't be buying anything.)

| English | Portuguese |
|---------|------------|
| So | De modo que |
| So | De maneira que |
| So that | De forma que |
| That | Que |

## 7) Comparative

Comparative conjunctions establish a relationship of comparison. For instance:

– A minha namorada é linda **como** uma princesa. (My girlfriend is beautiful as a princess.)

– As escolas fecharam, **ao passo que** as igrejas ficaram abertas. (Schools closed, whereas churches stayed open.)

| English | Portuguese |
|---------|------------|
| As | Como |
| As | Conforme |
| As well as | Assim como |
| As if | Como se |
| Whereas | Ao passo que |
| As well as | Bem como |

## 8) Integrating

Integrating conjunctions establish a relationship of completion. The subordinate clause completes the meaning of the main clause. For instance:

– Não sei **se** devo fazer o que tu dizes. (I don't know if I should do what you say.)

– A Maria disse **que** não vinha. (Maria said that she wouldn't be coming.)

| English | Portuguese |
|---------|------------|
| For | Para |
| That | Que |
| If | Se |

# 7.3 Vocabulary

## 7.3.1 Meals

A table with every meal of the day... Not literally, of course!

| English | Portuguese |
|---------|------------|
| Breakfast | Pequeno-almoço |
| Lunch | Almoço |
| Supper | Ceia |
| Dinner | Jantar |
| Meal | Refeição |

| English | Portuguese |
|---|---|
| Food | Comida |
| Drink | Bebida |
| Snack | Lanche |

### 7.3.2 Expressing likes & dislikes

The following expressions will be important for when you are eating out, but not exclusively – these are great ways to talk about what interests you and what doesn't.

| English | Portuguese |
|---|---|
| I like... | Eu gosto... |
| I love... | Eu amo... |
| I adore... | Eu adoro... |
| I'm crazy about... | Sou maluco por... |
| I'm mad about... | Sou doido por... |
| I enjoy... | Eu aprecio... |
| I have a soft spot for... | Eu tenho um fraco por... |
| I'm interested in... | Eu estou interessado em... |
| I'm in love with... | Eu estou apaixonado por... |
| I have a crush on... | Eu tenho uma panca por... |
| I hate... | Eu odeio... |

| | |
|---|---|
| I can't bear... | Eu não consigo suportar... |
| I detest... | Eu detesto... |
| It's not my cup of tea. | Não faz o meu tipo. |
| It's not my style. | Não faz o meu estilo. |
| That doesn't look good. | Isso não me parece bem. |
| I can't stand | Eu não consigo aguentar. |

### 7.3.3 Interjections

Here are some ways of politely interjecting (there are no swear words in this list!) But don't worry about it – I'm sure you know that those are the first words any native teaches somebody who is trying to learn a new language, so you'll get to hear them in no time.

| English | Portuguese |
|---|---|
| Ai! | Ai! |
| Enough! | Basta! |
| Dang! | Caraças! |
| *no equivalent* | Fogo![30] |
| Good! | Boa! |
| Let's go! | Vamos! |

---

30 "Fogo" literally means "Fire"!

| Yes sir! | Sim senhor! |
|---|---|
| Let's go! | Bora![31] |
| Congratulations! | Parabéns! |
| Go for it! | Força![32] |
| Gee! | Bolas! |
| My God! | Meu Deus! |
| Heavens! | Céus! |
| Jesus! | Credo! |
| Thank God! | Graças a Deus! |
| I wish! | Tomara! |
| If God wills! | Se Deus quiser! |
| I wish! | Quem me dera! |
| I'll be a monkey's uncle! | Macacos me mordam![33] |
| Nice! | Bem! |

---

31 "Bora" is the abbreviation of the bigger sentence "Vamos embora."

32 "Força" literally means "Strength."

33 Literally, this interjection translates to "Let monkeys bite me!"

# 7.4 Dining etiquette

Eating out in a different country might either be no big deal or just plain daunting, depending on the culture of the country in question. With that being said, countries in western Europe, and Portugal in particular, are not that different from the United States or the rest of the western world when it comes to dining etiquette. That also applies to Brazil. There are, however, a few differences that might be worth mentioning so that you positively impress your hosts if you ever find yourself being invited to a meal in a Portuguese or Brazilian home.

Let's begin with the common table manners: chewing with your mouth open and talking with your mouth full should be avoided; saying "Com licença (Excuse me)" or "Desculpe (Sorry)" when reaching across someone to grab something is encouraged. Also, you should thank anytime somebody brings, offers, or serves you something.

Whenever you get to the table, you should remain standing until invited to sit down – since usually, your host will show you to your seat. Typically, the host will seat at the head of the table, and if it is a couple, they each sit at the opposite ends of the table.

Don't expect grace to be said before meals, as it's not common, even though the most predominant religion in both Portugal and Brazil is Roman Catholicism. When seated at the table, the host will typically serve every guest, and only after everyone is served will the host serve themselves. Don't reach a bowl to serve yourself first since that is considered bad manners.

After everyone is served, the host will then usually say, "Bom apetite!" (Enjoy!) to signal everyone should start eating, or they might just pick up their utensils and start. Either way, never start eating before the hosts or before everyone at the table is served, even if someone is already eating. People might tell you to start so that your food doesn't get cold, but you should politely refuse. Whenever the host gives the signal, you can respond with a "Obrigado/a (Thank you)" or with another "Bom apetite" directed at the whole table.

When eating, forks are held with the left hand and knives with the right. You should not eat the main meal just with the fork in the right hand. Also, the utensils should never be pointed up. It's okay to take a break from holding the utensils, in which case the utensils should rest on the plate in the same position as you hold them.

If you do take a break, your hands should never be under the table, and if you need to rest, lean them on the table by their wrists and never by the elbow. When done eating, the knife should rest on the plate as it would be if you were taking a break, while the fork goes right below it.

# Chapter 8: At the Movies

« *Wow, my solo experience went great! I'm now feeling more confident about my Portuguese. What should I do next? I'm getting excited about the future and all its possibilities! Ok, I know: I'm going to the movies. Still, yesterday's lesson left me thinking about grammar, namely* **unisex nouns**, **adverbs of affirmation**, **negation and doubt**, *and* **future tense for regular and irregular verbs***... That's a lot to tackle! I better do a quick browser search in order to get it right.*

*Adverbs of negation*

*Adverbs of doubt*

*Future tense for regular & irregular verbs* »

"*Boas! Quero comprar um bilhete de cinema, por favor.*"

"*Boa noite! Que filme queres ver?*"

"*Erm... Sorry, I still didn't get to that part in my studies...*"

"No worries. Movies won't start until half-past nine, so since there's still some time left, do you want me to teach you a few sentences?"

"Yes please! This is unbelievable - you just read my thoughts. It just seems somebody is writing all of this!"

## 8.1 Movie time

Choosing a movie from a schedule and buying a ticket might seem challenging, but with all you know by now, it's something you will be able to learn in a heartbeat. Let's see how a conversation between a customer and an employee would go, starting from where we left off:

"Que filmes têm legendas em inglês? (Which movies have subtitles in English?)"

"Na verdade, todos os filmes estão na sua língua original, e têm legendas em português. Temos um filme em francês, oito em inglês, e um – para crianças – só em português. (Actually, all movies are in their original language, and have subtitles in Portuguese. We have a movie in French, eight in English, and one – for children – in Portuguese.)"

"Isso é perfeito. E que tipos de filme são? (That is perfect. And what type of movies are they?)"

*"Temos dois dramas, uma comédia, um filme de terror, um documentário francês, três filmes de acção, um de ficção científica e outro para crianças. (We have two dramas, a comedy, a horror movie, a French documentary, three action movies, a science-fiction one and another for children.)"*

*"E quanto custa um bilhete? (And how much is a ticket?)"*

*"Custa 5,50€. (It costs 5,50€.)"*

*"Então quero um bilhete para o filme de comédia, por favor. Pode dar-me também um pacote de pipocas doces e salgadas? (Then I want a ticket for the comedy movie, please. Can you also give me a bucket of sweet and salty popcorn?)"*

*"Claro. Aqui está o seu bilhete – o filme é na sala 4. E aqui estão as pipocas. Desfrute! (Sure. Here is your ticket – the movie is in room 4. And here is your popcorn. Enjoy!)"*

*"Muito obrigado! Tenha um bom dia! (Thank you very much. Have a nice day!)"*

# 8.2 Grammar

### 8.2.1 Unisex nouns

We already went through the gender of nouns, but you might remember that there are nouns that are unisex. What this means is that even though they have a defined gender (don't forget that every noun in Portuguese has a gender), they only have one form. In this larger group of unisex nouns, there are two smaller groups: one that consists of nouns that have a defined gender that isn't variableand another that consists of nouns that are variable in gender but only by the determinant that precedes. Let's make things clearer with some examples.

## One gender, one form

These nouns are usually the nouns pertaining to objects or things, which makes sense since they have no biological gender. To identify which words are masculine or feminine, you could follow what, at this point, should be a familiar rule – if it ends with an "O" it should be masculine, and if it ends with an "A," it should be feminine. Case in point:

- **A** mes**a**. (The table.)
- **O** garf**o**. (The fork)
- **O** vidr**o**. (The glass.)
- **A** canet**a**. (The pen.)

However, as you very well know by now, there are exceptions to this rule:

- **A** trib**o**. (The tribe.)
- **O** pijam**a**. (The pajamas.)
- **O** dilemma. (The dilemma.)

The other rules studied in chapter 2 also apply. So, nouns ending in "ÃO," "OR," "EU," and "ÊS" are usually masculine, while nouns ending in "Ã," "ORA," "OA," "ONA," "EIA," and "ESA" are usually feminine.

In these cases, if you are reading a text, you can always identify the gender of the noun by the preceding article. But if you are writing or speaking, there is no trick – you just have to study and memorize the correct gender.

## Two genders, one form

As for nouns in this group, they can either be masculine or feminine, but the word itself never changes. What changes is the article that precedes it, and only that. As an example:

- O / a artista (The male/female artist)
- O / a jovem (The young man/woman)
- O / a estudante (The male/female student)
- O / a cliente (The male/female client)
- O /a  gerente (The male/female manager.)

In these cases, the article preceding is really the key – it's the only way to identify the gender –  since the ending of the noun doesn't matter at all.

However, the ending can matter for one other thing – to identify if a noun is in the group. So, usually, nouns ending in "E" or "ISTA" belong to this sub-group of unisex nouns. Several of them are related to jobs and professions, but not all.

For instance, "FADISTA (singer of fado[34])" and "JORNALISTA (journalist)" are professions, while "TURISTA (tourist)" is not.

### 8.2.2 Adverbs of affirmation, negation, and doubt

Finally, the final round of adverbs. Once again, but for the last time, adverbs function as an information provider about the verb, adjective, or another adverb.

## Adverbs of affirmation

Adverbs of affirmation are inserted into a sentence to make an affirmative statement. Take a look at a few examples:

| Advérbios de afirmação | |
| --- | --- |
| Certainly | Certamente |
| Effectively | Efectivamente |

---

34 Fado is a traditional Portuguese music style.

| | |
|---|---|
| Really | Realmente |
| Surely | Decerto |
| Yes | Sim |

## Adverbs of negation

The adverbs of negation, also denial, are inserted in phrases in order to deny a statement. Take a look at a few examples:

| Advérbios de negação | |
|---|---|
| Neither | Nem |
| Never | Nunca |
| Never ever | Jamais |
| No | Não |
| Nor, neither | Tampouco |

## Adverbs of doubt

The adverbs of doubt or hesitation function as an indication of doubt within a sentence. Take a look at a few examples:

| Advérbios de dúvida | |
|---|---|
| Apparently | Aparentemente |
| Maybe | Talvez |
| Perhaps | Quiçá |

| | |
|---|---|
| Possibly | Possivelmente |
| Probably | Provavelmente |
| Suposedly | Supostamente |

### 8.2.3 Future tense for regular & irregular verbs

We already have gone through some verbs in the future tense (of the indicative mood), but it's time for a more thorough look[35]. In chapter 4, you learned about the present tense of regular verbs and how there are some rules you can follow to conjugate them depending on the ending of the verb. In the future tense, there is also a rule, which actually only has three exceptions. But the difference is that the rule applies to regular and irregular verbs.

So, the rule is that for you to conjugate a verb in the future tense, you just need to add the endings "EI," "ÁS," "Á," "EMOS," "EIS," and "ÃO" to the verb in its infinitive form (base form).

Let's take a look at all the verbs (both regular and irregular) that were conjugated in chapter 4 (4.2.4) and chapter 5 (5.2.2 and 5.2.4) and conjugate them in the future tense.

| Verbo AMAR (to love) | |
|---|---|
| Eu | Amarei |
| Tu | Amarás |
| Ele/a | Amará |
| Nós | Amaremos |

---

[35] You should know, however, that the future tense is used more often in writing than in speech.

---

| Vós | Ama**reis** |
|---|---|
| Eles/as | Ama**rão** |

## Verbo VIVER (to live)

| Eu | Viverei |
|---|---|
| Tu | Viverás |
| Ele/a | Viverá |
| Nós | Viveremos |
| Vós | Vivereis |
| Eles/as | Viverão |

## Verbo PARTIR (to break)

| Eu | Partirei |
|---|---|
| Tu | Partirás |
| Ele/a | Partirá |
| Nós | Partiremos |
| Vós | Partireis |

| Eles/as | Partirão |
|---------|----------|

## Verbo PÔR (to put)

| Eu | Porei |
|---------|----------|
| Tu | Porás |
| Ele/a | Porá |
| Nós | Poremos |
| Vós | Poreis |
| Eles/as | Porão |

## Verbo PODER (to can)

| Eu | Poderei |
|---------|----------|
| Tu | Poderás |
| Ele/a | Poderá |
| Nós | Poderemos |
| Vós | Podereis |
| Eles/as | Poderão |

## Verbo DAR (to give)

| Eu | Darei |
|---|---|
| Tu | Darás |
| Ele/a | Dará |
| Nós | Daremos |
| Vós | Dareis |
| Eles/as | Darão |

## Verbo VIR (to come)

| Eu | Virei |
|---|---|
| Tu | Virás |
| Ele/a | Virá |
| Nós | Viremos |
| Vós | Vireis |
| Eles/as | Virão |

## Verbo FALAR (to speak)

| Eu | Falarei |
|---|---|
| Tu | Falarás |
| Ele/a | Falará |
| Nós | Falaremos |
| Vós | Falareis |
| Eles/as | Falarão |

## Verbo QUERER (to want)

| Eu | Quererei |
|---|---|
| Tu | Quererás |
| Ele/a | Quererá |
| Nós | Quereremos |
| Vós | Querereis |
| Eles/as | Quererão |

## Verbo PEDIR (to ask)

| Eu | Pedirei |
|---|---|
| Tu | Pedirás |
| Ele/a | Pedirá |
| Nós | Pediremos |
| Vós | Pedireis |
| Eles/as | Pedirão |

## Verbo OUVIR (to listen)

| Eu | Ouvirei |
|---|---|
| Tu | Ouvirás |
| Ele/a | Ouvirá |
| Nós | Ouviremos |
| Vós | Ouvireis |
| Eles/as | Ouvirão |

## Verbo CABER (to fit)

| Eu | Caberei |
|---|---|
| Tu | Caberás |
| Ele/a | Caberá |
| Nós | Caberemos |
| Vós | Cabereis |
| Eles/as | Caberão |

## Verbo TER

| Eu | Terei |
|---|---|
| Tu | Terás |
| Ele/a | Terás |
| Nós | Teremos |
| Vós | Tereis |
| Eles/as | Terão |

## Verbo HAVER

| | |
|---|---|
| Eu | Haverei |
| Tu | Haverás |
| Ele/a | Haverá |
| Nós | Haveremos |
| Vós | Havereis |
| Eles/as | Haverão |

## Verbo SER

| | |
|---|---|
| Eu | Serei |
| Tu | Serás |
| Ele/a | Será |
| Nós | Seremos |
| Vós | Sereis |
| Eles/as | Serão |

So, what are the three exceptions? The verbs "FAZER (to do)," "TRAZER (to bring)," and "DIZER (to say)." However, even though these are the exceptions to the rule, the endings will still be the same – the difference is that they are added not to the infinitive form of the verb, but to the verb with the letters "ZER" dropped first. Check the following tables to see how you should conjugate these verbs:

| Verbo FAZER (to do) | |
|---|---|
| Eu | Far**ei** |
| Tu | Far**ás** |
| Ele/a | Far**á** |
| Nós | Far**emos** |
| Vós | Far**eis** |
| Eles/as | Far**ão** |

| Verbo TRAZER (to bring) | |
|---|---|
| Eu | Trarei |
| Tu | Trarás |
| Ele/a | Trará |
| Nós | Traremos |
| Vós | Trareis |
| Eles/as | Trarão |

| Verbo DIZER (to say) ||
| --- | --- |
| Eu | Direi |
| Tu | Dirás |
| Ele/a | Dirá |
| Nós | Diremos |
| Vós | Direis |
| Eles/as | Dirão |

# 8.3 Vocabulary

## 8.3.1 Telling the time & date

Unlike in the United States and many other countries around the world, the time format favored in Portugal is the 24-hour one. That means that when telling somebody the time, you should read out the exact hours and minutes shown on the clock. Even though the fully correct way of answering the question: "Que horas são? (What time is it?)" would be "São dezoito horas e trinta e dois minutos" (It's eighteen hours and thirty-two minutes), usually the words "horas" and "minutos" are omitted[36]. Check out the following examples of how to tell the time:

---

36 You might have noticed that when asking the time in Portuguese, the verb is in the plural form. That is always the case when telling the time in Portuguese, with only one exception: when it's one o'clock (*p.m.* or *a.m.*). In that case you should answer, for instance, "É uma hora e cinco minutos (03h05)."

| | |
|---|---|
| 13h15 | Treze e quinze[37] (thirteen and fifteen) |
| 15h30 | Quinze e trinta[38] |
| 16h45 | Dezasseis e quarenta e cinco[39] |
| 20h00 | Vinte[40] |
| 12h00 | Doze[41] (twelve o'clock) |
| 00h00 | Meia-noite (midnight) |

However, the 12-hour format is often used as well in more informal settings. In those scenarios, *a.m.* and *p.m.* are not used; instead, the expressions "da manhã (in the morning)," "da tarde (in the afternoon)," or "da noite (in the night)" are used. For instance:

| | |
|---|---|
| 13h16 | Uma e dezasseis da tarde |
| 15h30 | Três e trinta da tarde |

---

37 As fifteen minutes are a quarter of an hour, you can also say "Treze e um quarto (Thirteen and a quarter)."

38 Just like in English you could say "half past three," in Portuguese you can also say "Quinze e meia (Three and a half)."

39 Again, just like in English you could say "a quarter to five," in Portuguese it is also said "Quinze/um quarto para as dezassete." Plus, in northern regions of Portugal it is also commonly said "Dezassete menos um quarto (Five less a quarter)."

40 Usually, in these cases (eight on the dot, sharp), you accompany it by saying "Vinte horas" or "Vinte em ponto."

41 It can also be said "meio-dia (midday)."

| | |
|---|---|
| 16h53 | Quatro e cinquenta e três da tarde |
| 21h00 | Nove da noite |
| 2h00 | Duas da manhã |
| 11h00 | Onze da manhã |

When it comes to telling the date, first we have to get to know the days of the week:

| **English** | **Portuguese** |
|---|---|
| Monday | Segunda-feira |
| Tuesday | Terça-feira |
| Wednesday | Quarta-feira |
| Thursday | Quinta-feira |
| Friday | Sexta-feira |
| Saturday | Sábado |
| Sunday | Domingo |

Having learned the days of the week, we now need to know how to write the format itself. Either the number or the word format can be used. When it comes to the number format, instead of being **mm/dd/yy**, in Portuguese, it always goes **dd/mm/yyyy**. So, "*February 17, 2022 (9/17/22)*" would appear as "*17/09/2022.*"

The written format goes **day of the week, day of the month of the year**. So, again, "*Tuesday, February 17, 2022*" would be "*Terça-*

*feira, 17 de Fevereiro de 2022."*

## 8.3.2 Ordinal numerals

We have already learned about the cardinal numbers; now let's take a look at the ordinal numbers from 1 to 100:

| English | Portuguese |
|---|---|
| First | Primeiro |
| Second | Segundo |
| Third | Terceiro |
| Forth | Quarto |
| Fifth | Quinto |
| Sixth | Sexto |
| Seventh | Sétimo |
| Eighth | Oitavo |
| Ninth | Nono |
| Tenth | Décimo |
| Twentieth | Vigésimo |
| Thirtieth | Trigésimo |
| Fortieth | Quadragésimo |
| Fiftieth | Quinquagésimo |

| | |
|---|---|
| Sixtieth | Sexagésimo |
| Seventieth | Septagésimo |
| Eightieth | Octogésimo |
| Ninetieth | Nonagésimo |
| Hundredth | Centésimo |

You may ask: "What about the numbers in between?" Well, just like the cardinal numbers, you just need to add the ordinal number that you need from the first set of 10 in front of the number you already have. So, for instance:

| English | Portuguese |
|---|---|
| Twelfth | Décimo *segundo* |
| Twenty-seventh | Vigésimo *sétimo* |
| Thirty-first | Trigésimo *primeiro* |
| Forty-ninth | Quadragésimo *nono* |
| Fifty-sixth | Quinquagésimo *sexto* |

### 8.3.3 Describing people's personality

Having the vocabulary to describe people's personalities is crucial in order to add depth to a conversation. Here's a list of adjectives that do just that:

| English | Portuguese |
| --- | --- |
| Adventurous | Aventureira/o |
| Ambitious | Ambiciosa/o |
| Anxious | Ansiosa/o |
| Arrogant | Arrogante |
| Bad-tempered | Mau feitio |
| Bossy | Mandona/mandão |
| Calm | Calma/o |
| Careful | Cuidadosa/o |
| Careless | Descuidada/o |
| Cheerful | Animada/o |
| Confident | Confiante |
| Courageous | Corajosa/o |
| Crazy | Maluca/o |
| Creative | Criativa/o |
| Determined | Determinada/o |
| Discreet | Discreta/o |

| | |
|---|---|
| Dishonest | Desonesta/o |
| Distracted | Distraída/o |
| Emotional | Emotiva/o |
| Energetic | Energética/o |
| Faithful | Fiel |
| Fearless | Destemida/o |
| Friendly | Amigável |
| Funny | Engraçada/o |
| Generous | Generosa/o |
| Gentle | Gentil |
| Happy | Feliz |
| Hard-working | Trabalhador(a) |
| Helpful | Prestável |
| Honest | Honesta/o |
| Humble | Humilde |
| Hypocritical | Hipócrita |
| Impatient | Impaciente |

| | |
|---|---|
| Intelligent | Inteligente |
| Jealous | Invejosa/o |
| Kind | Boa/bom |
| Lazy | Preguiçosa/o |
| Loyal | Leal |
| Mean | Má/mau |
| Modest | Modesta/o |
| Nervous | Nervosa/o |
| Nice | Simpática/o |
| Optimistic | Optimista |
| Overbearing | Prepotente |
| Patient | Paciente |
| Persistent | Persistente |
| Pessimistic | Pessimista |
| Polite | Educada/o |
| Popular | Popular |
| Powerful | Poderosa/o |

| | |
|---|---|
| Proud | Orgulhosa/o |
| Rational | Racional |
| Reliable | Confiável |
| Romantic | Romântica/o |
| Rude | Rude |
| Selfish | Egoísta |
| Sensible | Razoável |
| Sensitive | Sensível |
| Serious | Séria/o |
| Shy | Tímida/o |
| Sincere | Sincera/o |
| Smart | Esperta/o |
| Sociable | Sociável |
| Stubborn | Teimosa/o |
| Talkative | Falador(a) |
| Worried | Preocupada/o |

# 8.4 Exercises

Grab your popcorn and sit comfortably, for it is movie time! The exercise in this chapter is a very fun one. All you need to do is to watch this recommended movie: "A Herdade (The Domain)," and then fill out the following character sheet with the **main** character's traits. This Portuguese movie, which was internationally acclaimed, portrays the life of a man and his family before and after the troubled times of the Carnation Revolution of 1974 up until the current day.

---

### CHARACTER SHEET

Name:_____

Age:_____

Gender: _____

Occupation:_____

Marital status: _____

Physical Appearance:

- _____

- _____

- _____

Personality:

- _____

- _____

- _____

# Chapter 9: Talking about the Past

> « What a blast that was! I'm really going to miss Portugal when I leave... But I also miss my family and can't wait to see them. I'm going to rant nonstop about my time in Lisbon: where I've been, what I learned, who I've met... But what if I do it in Portuguese? True that they wouldn't be able to understand me, but I'll leave that problem for future Tom to solve. Right now, I need to learn how to talk about the past. Hmm... **past tenses for regular and irregular verbs**, **indefinite pronouns** and **relative pronouns?** Seems like I found the perfect lesson for today. »

## 9.1 The past

They say to not dwell on the past, but the truth is that remembering the past, talking about the past, and learning from the past is a crucial part of our development as a person. It is also the backbone of our identity, what gives us a story. So, it only makes sense that when you are learning a new language, you learn how to do it in order to be able to talk about yourself - about who you have been, where, and what you did, among many other things. Of course, learning to talk about the past also encompasses being able to tell somebody what you ate for breakfast yesterday morning – and that is, perhaps, even a bigger deal!

With that in mind, check out the following dialogue that focuses on talking about past events:

*"Que bom estar de volta! Tinha muitas saudades vossas! (How nice to be back! I missed you very much!)"*

*"Nós também sentimos a tua falta. Como foram as férias? Onde estiveste? Onde foste? (We missed you too. How were your vacations? Where have you been? Where did you go to?)"*

*"Foram incríveis! Conheci pessoas novas, passeei muito por Lisboa... Enfim, tenho tanto para contar! (They were amazing! I met new people; I walked a lot around Lisbon... Well, I have so much to tell!)"*

*"Queremos saber tudo! (We want to know everything!)"*

*"Então, na viagem de avião li um panfleto que me introduziu à língua portuguesa; no avião conheci ainda um rapaz muito prestável chamado João que me ensinou umas coisas. Depois de fazer check-in no hotel, fui comprar estes presentes para vocês - gostam? (So, on the*

*airplane ride I read a pamphlet that introduced me to the Portuguese language; still on the plane I met a very helpful guy named João who taught me a few things. After checking-in at the hotel, I went to buy these gifts for you – do you like them?)"*

*"São lindos, muito obrigada! Mas continua a contar-nos como foi! (They are beautiful, thank you very much! But continue telling us how it went!)"*

*"Nos dias seguintes andei por Lisboa a conhecer a cidade e os monumentos históricos. E, claro, sempre a estudar e a absorver Português. Foi num desses dias que conheci uma guia – a Marta – que agora é minha amiga, e que me convidou para jantar na casa dela. (The next few days I walked around Lisbon getting to know the town and its historical monuments. And of course, always studying, and absorbing Portuguese. It was on one of those days that I met a guide – Marta – who is my friend now, who invited me to dinner at her place.)"*

*"Só tu e ela? (Only you and her?)"*

*"Não, estava lá a família e amigos dela. E eram todos muitos simpáticos. Visitei ainda restaurantes típicos onde comi comida regional, e até sobrou tempo para ir ao cinema! (No, her family and friends were there. And they were all really nice. I also visited typical restaurants, in which I ate regional food, and I still had time left to go to the movies!)"*

*"Então foram umas férias para repetir? (So, they were holidays to repeat?)"*

*"Sem dúvida. Estou morto por voltar lá - e com vocês todos da próxima vez! (Without a doubt. I'm dying to go back there - and with all of you next time!)"*

## 9.2 Grammar

### 9.2.1 Past tenses for regular & irregular verbs

We have already discussed the present and future tenses of both regular and irregular verbs. So, the only tense left to study is the past tense. The previous dialogue might have introduced you to a lot of talking about the past, but now we are going to take a look at a few rules.

In Portuguese, and as we said in chapter 5 (5.2.3), in the indicative mood, we have three past tenses: the perfect indicative (simple past), imperfect indicative (or past continuous), and pluperfect. In this chapter, we are going to focus on the most common past tenses - the simple past and the past continuous - which are used daily in any conversation, thus making it essential to learn them.

# Simple Past (perfect indicative)

As in English, the simple past is used to indicate an action that occurred in a determined moment of the past, often a single event that has come and gone – it's a one-time action.

So, to conjugate regular verbs ending in "AR" in the simple past, after the stem, you just need to add – "EI," "ASTE," "OU," "ÁMOS," "ASTES," and "ARAM." For instance:

| Verbo AMAR (to love) ||
| --- | --- |
| Eu | Amei |
| Tu | Amaste |
| Ele/a | Amou |
| Nós | Am**á**mos |
| Vós | Amastes |
| Eles/as | Amaram |

When it comes to conjugating regular verbs ending in "ER" in the simple past, after the stem, you just need to add – "I," "ESTE," "EU," "EMOS," "ESTES," and "ERAM." For instance:

| Verbo VIVER (to live) ||
| --- | --- |
| Eu | Vivi |
| Tu | Viveste |

| | |
|---|---|
| Ele/a | Viveu |
| Nós | Vivemos |
| Vós | Vivestes |
| Eles/as | Viveram |

Lastly, with verbs ending in "IR" after the stem, you just need to add – "I," "ISTE," "IU," "IMOS," "ISTES," and "IRAM." For instance:

| Verbo PARTIR (to break) | |
|---|---|
| Eu | Parti |
| Tu | Partiste |
| Ele/a | Partiu |
| Nós | Partimos |
| Vós | Partistes |
| Eles/as | Partiram |

# Past Continuous (imperfect indicative)

The past continuous is used to indicate an action that wasn't concluded (imperfect, unfinished); something that happened in the past that was ongoing. If the simple past is used for one-time events, the past continuous is used for describing habits, for instance, or for actions that happened in the past that don't have a clear endpoint.

Once again, there are patterns to follow depending on whether the verbs end in "AR," "ER," or "IR." And, of course, that applies only to regular verbs.

So, when it comes to conjugating regular verbs ending in "ER" in the past continuous, after the stem, you just need to add – "AVA," "AVAS," "AVA," "ÁVAMOS," "ÁVES," and "AVAM." For instance:

| Verbo AMAR (to love) | |
|---|---|
| Eu | Amava |
| Tu | Amavas |
| Ele/a | Amava |
| Nós | Amávamos |
| Vós | Amáveis |
| Eles/as | Amavam |

When it comes to conjugating regular verbs ending in "ER" and "IR" in the continuous past, after the stem, you just need to add – "IA," "IAS," "IA," "ÍAMOS," "ÍEIS," and "IAM." For instance:

| Verbo VIVER (to live) | |
|---|---|
| Eu | Vivia |
| Tu | Vivias |
| Ele/a | Vivia |
| Nós | Vivíamos |
| Vós | Vivíeis |

| Eles/as | Viviam |
|---------|--------|

| Verbo PARTIR (to break) | |
|---------|--------|
| Eu | Partia |
| Tu | Partias |
| Ele/a | Partia |
| Nós | Partíamos |
| Vós | Partíeis |
| Eles/as | Partiam |

# Irregular verbs

This all might have seemed like a lot of information to handle; however, once you practice a little bit, the different rules for the three verb endings in the different tenses will come out of you almost automatically. You can always make a song out of it and recite the verbs out loud to make it catchier and easier for your brain to absorb when conjugating verbs.

Nevertheless, when it comes to irregular verbs, there aren't many tricks in the book besides old and simple memorization. Sure, you can try different memorization techniques, but there are no rules to rely on, really. So, the following are some of the most common irregular verbs conjugated in both tenses we have just studied.

## Verbo TER

|  | Simple past | Past continuous |
| --- | --- | --- |
| Eu | Tive | Tinha |
| Tu | Tiveste | Tinhas |
| Ele/a | Teve | Tinha |
| Nós | Tivemos | Tínhamos |
| Vós | Tivestes | Tínheis |
| Eles/as | Tiveram | Tinham |

## Verbo HAVER

|  | Simple past | Past continuous |
| --- | --- | --- |
| Eu | Houve | Havia |
| Tu | Houveste | Havias |
| Ele/a | Houve | Havia |
| Nós | Houvemos | Havíamos |
| Vós | Houvestes | Havíeis |

| Eles/as | Houveram | Haviam |
|---|---|---|

| Verbo SER | | |
|---|---|---|
| | **Simple past** | **Past continuous** |
| Eu | Fui | Era |
| Tu | Foste | Eras |
| Ele/a | Foi | Era |
| Nós | Fomos | Éramos |
| Vós | Fostes | Éreis |
| Eles/as | Foram | Eram |

| Verbo ESTAR | | |
|---|---|---|
| | **Simple past** | **Past continuous** |
| Eu | Estive | Estava |
| Tu | Estiveste | Estavas |
| Ele/a | Esteve | Estava |
| Nós | Estivemos | Estávamos |

| | | |
|---|---|---|
| Vós | Estivestes | Estáveis |
| Eles/as | Estiveram | Estavam |

| Verbo FICAR | | |
|---|---|---|
| | **Simple past** | **Past continuous** |
| Eu | Fiquei | Ficava |
| Tu | Ficaste | Ficavas |
| Ele/a | Ficou | Ficava |
| Nós | Ficámos | Ficávamos |
| Vós | Ficastes | Ficáveis |
| Eles/as | Ficaram | Ficavam |

| Verbo IR | | |
|---|---|---|
| | **Simple past** | **Past continuous** |
| Eu | Fui | Ia |
| Tu | Foste | Ias |
| Ele/a | Foi | Ia |

| | | |
|---|---|---|
| Nós | Fomos | Íamos |
| Vós | Fostes | Íeis |
| Eles/as | Foram | Iam |

### 9.2.2 Indefinite pronouns

Indefinite pronouns are pronouns that refer to nouns in a vague, imprecise, generic way – rather, in an undefined way. When you can't really be precise about whom or what you are talking about, these are the pronouns that you will use.

In Portuguese, there are variable and invariable pronouns. Variable pronouns can change according to gender and number, while invariable pronouns don't. The following are the indefinite pronouns in the Portuguese language:

| Pronomes Indefinidos | |
|---|---|
| **Variable** | **invariable** |
| Algum, alguma, alguns, algumas (some / any / a few) | Alguém (someone / somebody) |
| Nenhum, nenhuma, nenhuns, nenhumas (none) | Ninguém (no one, nobody) |
| Todo, toda, todos, todas (all) | Tudo (everything) |
| Outro, outra, outros, outras (other) | Outrem (other) |
| Muito, muita, muitos, muitas (many) | Nada (nothing) |

| | |
|---|---|
| Pouco, pouca, poucos, poucas (few) | Quem (whoever) |
| Certo, certa, certos, certas (certain) | Cada (each / every) |
| Vários, várias (several) | Algo (something) |
| Tanto, tanta, tantos, tantas (as many) | |
| Quanto, quanta, quantos, quantas (how many) | |
| Qualquer, quaisquer (any / anything) | |

Let's take a look at a few of these pronouns used in sentences:

– **Algo** se passa! (Something is up!)

– Ele não está a esconder **nada.** (He is not hiding anything.)

– **Alguém** esteve aqui? (Was someone here?)

– **Certo** dia fui passear. (A certain day, I went walking.)

– A árvore tem **poucas** folhas. (The tree has few leaves.)

– Nós comemos **qualquer** coisa. (We eat anything.)

### 9.2.3 Relative pronouns

Relative pronouns are the ones that represent nouns already mentioned previously in the sentence and to which they *relate* to, thus creating a subordinate sentence that is dependent on the first part of the phrase. Bit confusing, right? Well, check out the following example:

> – A bailarina está ali. A bailarina é muito alta. (The ballerina is over there. The ballerina is very tall.)

These two sentences can be independent but are too repetitive if separate. So, we can connect them:

- - A bailarina *que* está ali é muito alta. (The ballerina that/who is over there is very tall.)
- Now the sentence is connected, and the word that built that bridge was the relative pronoun "QUE (that)," which refers to the noun "BAILARINA (ballerina)." Check out another example:
- Comi ontem uns chocolates. Comprei os chocolates on-line. (Yesterday, I ate some chocolate. I bought the chocolate on-line.)
- And now connected:
- Comi ontem uns chocolates, *os quais* comprei on-line. (Yesterday, I ate some chocolate, which I bought on-line.)

The following are all the relative pronouns in the Portuguese language:

| Pronomes Relativos | |
|---|---|
| **Variable** | **Invariable** |
| O qual, a qual, os quais, as quais | Quem |
| Cujo, cuja, cujos, cujas | Que |
| Quanto, quanta, quantos, quantas | Onde |

# 9.3 Vocabulary

## 9.3.1 Time expressions for past events

To talk about the past, these expressions are essential!

| English | Portuguese |
|---|---|
| A few days ago | Uns dias atrás |
| Last Sunday | Último domingo |
| Last week | Na semana passada |
| Last year | Ano passado |
| Some time ago | Um tempo atrás |
| The day before yesterday | Anteontem |
| Yesterday | Ontem |
| Yesterday night | Ontem à noite |

## 9.3.2 Months & Seasons

Knowing the names of the months and the season of the year is fundamental to speaking any language. Here is a table to help you with that:

| English | Portuguese |
|---|---|
| Months | Meses |
| January | Janeiro |

| February | Fevereiro |
| --- | --- |
| March | Março |
| April | Abril |
| May | Maio |
| June | Junho |
| July | Julho |
| August | Agosto |
| September | Setembro |
| October | Outubro |
| November | Novembro |
| December | Dezembro |
| Spring | Primavera |
| Summer | Verão |
| Autumn/Fall | Outono |
| Winter | Inverno |
| Easter | Páscoa |
| Christmas | Natal |

| English | Portuguese |
|---------|------------|
| Christmas Eve | Véspera de Natal/Consoada |
| New Year | Ano Novo |
| New Year's Eve | Véspera de Ano Novo |
| April Fool's Day | Dia das Mentiras |
| Halloween | Dia das Bruxas |

### 9.3.3 Jobs & Professions

If your answer to the question "What do you want to do when you grow up?" is "To know several names of jobs and professions in Portuguese," here is a table that helps you fulfill that dream:

| English | Portuguese |
|---------|------------|
| Accountant | Contabilista |
| Actress | Actor/actriz |
| Archaeologist | Arqueólogo/a |
| Architect | Arquitecto/a |
| Ballet dancer | Bailarino/a |
| Bank clerk | Bancário/a |
| Biologist | Biólogo/a |
| Chemist | Químico/a |
| Doctor | Médico/a |

| | |
|---|---|
| Engineer | Engenheiro/a |
| Firefighter | Bombeiro/a |
| Hairstylist | Cabeleireiro/a |
| Judge | Juíz(a) |
| Lawyer | Advogado/a |
| Mechanic | Mecânico/a |
| Nurse | Enfermeiro/a |
| Painter | Pintor(a) |
| Poet | Poeta/poetisa |
| Psychologist | Psicólogo/a |
| Saleswoman | Vendedor(a) |
| Singer | Cantor(a) |
| Student | Aluno/a |
| Surgeon | Cirurgião/ã |
| Teacher | Professor(a) |
| Veterinarian | Veterinário/a |
| Writer | Escritor(a) |

# 9.4 Quiz

You have now almost reached the end of this book, so it is time for another quiz test! This test will encompass the most important materials you have studied, starting from chapter 6 up until 9. And like the quiz in chapter 5, this too will have a score in the end. The score works like this: out of a total of 140 points, you must score 70 points to pass. Each right answer is worth one point.

If you don't pass, don't let it get you down. Just go back to the chapters where you struggled the most, re-read those and study them so that you can master all of that knowledge once and for all. Good luck!

1) **Identify only the direct object in the following sentences and substitute it for the correct pronoun.**

- Eu emprestei a caneta. (I lent my pen.)

- A Rita e a Leonor fazem os trabalhos de casa. (Rita and Leonor do their homework.)

- Eu não quero chocolate. (I don't want chocolate.)

- Ele vai dar um presente à namorada. (He will give a gift to his girlfriend.)

- Quem contou o meu segredo? (Who told my secret?)

- A Rita e a Leonor também fazem os trabalhos de casa. (Rita and Leonor also do their homework.)

2) **Identify only the indirect object in the following sentences and substitute it for the correct pronoun.**

- A Teresa estragou a cama à irmã. (Teresa ruined her sister's bed.)

- O cão sujou o chão do meu vizinho. (The dog stained my neighbor's floor.)

- Ele vai dar um presente à namorada. (He will give a gift to the girlfriend.)

- O meu pai queria abraçar a ti. (My father wanted to hug you.)

- Os ladrões queriam fazer mal a nós. (The thieves wanted to hurt us.)

- Elas fizeram as malas das filhas. (They packed their daughter's suitcases.)

3) **Now substitute the direct and indirect object for the correct pronouns.**

- Ele vai dar um presente à namorada. (He will give a gift to the girlfriend.)

- A Teresa estragou a cama à irmã. (Teresa ruined her sister's bed.)

- A Rita e a Leonor também fazem os trabalhos de casa da Inês. (Rita and Leonor also do Inês' homework.)

- O presidente ofereceu um prémio a ti. (The president offered a prize to you.)

4) **Fill out the blank spaces in the following table with the adjective adapted to the correspondent gender.**

| English | Masculine | Feminine |
|---|---|---|
| Arrogant | Arrogante | |
| Bald | | Careca |
| Bossy | Mandão | |
| Champion | Campeão | |
| Charming | | Encantadora |
| Commoner | | Plebeia |
| Confident | Confiante | |
| Conservative | Conservador | |
| Courteous | Cortês | |
| English | | Inglesa |

| English | Portuguese (col 2) | Portuguese (col 3) |
|---|---|---|
| European | Europeu | |
| Faithful | Fiel | |
| Generous | Generoso | |
| Gentle | | Gentil |
| Healthy | São | |
| Hideous | Horrendo | |
| Idiot | | Idiota |
| Intelligent | Inteligente | |
| Muscular | Musculado | |
| Naked | | Nua |
| Orphan | | Orfã |
| Raw | Cru | |
| Romantic | | Romântica |
| Rude | Rude | |
| Sociable | Sociável | |
| Stubborn | Teimoso | |
| Talkative | Falador | |

| Tanned | | Bronzeada |
|--------|--|-----------|

5) Underline the possessive adjectives in the sentences below and fill the blank spaces with the correct possessive pronouns.

- O meu cão não tem coleira. Este tem, logo deve ser o _____. (My dog doesn't have a leash. This one has, so it must be ...)

- A tua casa é enorme! A _____ é tão pequena... (Your house is enormous! _____ is so small...)

- O professor disse que esta são as vossas guitarras. É verdade que são _____? (The professor said that these are your guitars. Is it true that they are _____?)

- Se eu tenho um problema, o problema não é teu, é _____. (If I have a problema, it's not your problem, it's _____.)

6) Conjugate the following verbs in the future tense of the indicative mood.

| Verbo IR | |
|----------|--|
| Eu | |
| Tu | |
| Ele/a | |
| Nós | |
| Vós | |
| Eles/as | |

| Verbo FICAR | |
|---|---|
| Eu | |
| Tu | |
| Ele/a | |
| Nós | |
| Vós | |
| Eles/as | |

| Verbo ESTAR | |
|---|---|
| Eu | |
| Tu | |
| Ele/a | |
| Nós | |
| Vós | |
| Eles/as | |

7) Underline the verbs conjugated in the past tense (perfect and imperfect indicative) in the dialogue found in the beginning of chapter 9.

8) Conjugate the following verbs in the <u>simple past tense of the</u> <u>indicative mood.</u>

| Verbo ANDAR (to walk) | |
|---|---|
| Eu | |
| Tu | |
| Ele/a | |
| Nós | |
| Vós | |
| Eles/as | |

| Verbo COMER (to eat) | |
|---|---|
| Eu | |
| Tu | |
| Ele/a | |
| Nós | |
| Vós | |
| Eles/as | |

| Verbo **SENTIR** (to feel) | |
|---|---|
| Eu | |
| Tu | |
| Ele/a | |
| Nós | |
| Vós | |
| Eles/as | |

9) Conjugate the following verbs in the <u>past continuous of the</u> <u>indicative mood.</u>

| Verbo **OLHAR** (to look) | |
|---|---|
| Eu | |
| Tu | |
| Ele/a | |
| Nós | |
| Vós | |
| Eles/as | |

## Verbo SABER (to know)

| | |
|---|---|
| Eu | |
| Tu | |
| Ele/a | |
| Nós | |
| Vós | |
| Eles/as | |

## Verbo SORRIR (to smile)

| | |
|---|---|
| Eu | |
| Tu | |
| Ele/a | |
| Nós | |
| Vós | |
| Eles/as | |

# Chapter 10: Basic Grammar Revision

Congratulations, you have made it to the end of the book! You should be proud of yourself!

Now it's time for a language-learning victory lap: no new information or further explanations in this chapter – just as the title says, it's a basic revision for you to refresh most of the grammar material that you learned throughout, all condensed in one chapter. It will be filled with the main information, plus charts and tables that were presented previously, which you can now consult here without having to go through all of the chaff.

## Word order

In a declarative statement, it goes 1) SUBJECT + 2) VERB + 3) OBJECT / COMPLEMENT (when there is one).

| | |
|---|---|
| I eat bread. | Eu como pão. |
| He drinks water. | Ele bebe água. |
| You are men. | Vocês são homens. |

In descriptive sentences, the adjective usually follows the noun instead of preceding it:

| | |
|---|---|
| Your **yellow** car is broken. | O teu carro **amarelo** está partido. |
| He is a **big** man. | Ele é um homem **grande**. |
| They have a **small** house. | Eles têm uma casa **pequena**. |

In negative statements, the word "NÃO" (not) is placed before the verb and that's enough to turn an affirmative statement into a negative one:

| English | PT - affirmative | PT - negative |
|---|---|---|
| I like you. | Eu gosto de ti. | Eu **não** gosto de ti. |
| She stole my bike. | Ela roubou a minha bicicleta. | Ela **não** roubou a minha bicicleta. |

In interrogative statements, unlike in English, there is no need to switch the order between the subject and the verb. A statement turns into a question by merely adding a question mark at the end of a sentence and rising the intonation of the phrase.

| | |
|---|---|
| The ball is yours. | A bola é tua. |
| Is the ball yours? | A bola é tua? |
| They are running. | Eles estão a correr. |
| Are they running? | Eles estão a correr? |

# Verb "TO BE" – verbs "SER" and "ESTAR"

The difference between them is that the verb "Ser" is usually the chosen one when it comes to talking about states that tend to be continuous and/or long-lasting throughout your lifetime. On the contrary, the verb "Estar" is used to refer to states that tend to be susceptible to changes.

| Verbo SER | |
|---|---|
| Eu | Sou |
| Tu | És |
| Ele/a | É |
| Nós | Somos |
| Vós | Sois |
| Eles/as | São |

| Verbo ESTAR | |
|---|---|
| Eu | Estou |
| Tu | Estás |
| Ele/a | Está |
| Nós | Estamos |
| Vós | Estais |

| Eles/as | Estão |
|---------|-------|

# Gender of nouns & adjectives

All nouns in Portuguese have gender. Luckily, many of the rules that apply to the gender of nouns also apply to the gender of adjectives. That's the case because many nouns can turn into adjectives and vice-versa.

Nouns ending in "O":

| English | Masculine | Feminine |
|---------|-----------|----------|
| Boyfriend/girlfriend | Namorad<u>o</u> | Namorad<u>a</u> |
| Cat | Gat<u>o</u> | Gat<u>a</u> |
| Cousin | Prim<u>o</u> | Prim<u>a</u> |
| Friend | Amig<u>o</u> | Amig<u>a</u> |

Adjectives ending in "O"

| English | Masculine | Feminine |
|---------|-----------|----------|
| Beautiful | Bonit<u>o</u> | Bonit<u>a</u> |
| Tall | Alt<u>o</u> | Alt<u>a</u> |
| Thin | Magr<u>o</u> | Magr<u>a</u> |
| Stupid | Estúpid<u>o</u> | Estúpid<u>a</u> |

## Nouns ending in "ÃO":

| English | Masculine | Feminine |
|---|---|---|
| Captain | Capit**ão** | Capit**ã** |
| Surgeon | Cirurgi**ão** | Cirurgi**ã** |
| Lion / Lioness | Le**ão** | Le**oa** |
| Boss | Patr**ão** | Patr**oa** |
| Glutton | Glut**ão** | Gluto**na** |
| Reveler | Foli**ão** | Foli**ona** |

## Adjectives ending in "ÃO"

| English | Masculine | Feminine |
|---|---|---|
| Healthy | S**ão** | S**ã** |
| Orphan | Orf**ão** | Orf**ã** |
| "Cry baby" | Chor**ão** | Chor**ona** |
| Swashbuckler | Fanfarr**ão** | Fanfarr**ona** |

Nouns ending in "OR":

| English | Masculine | Feminine |
|---------|-----------|----------|
| Driver | Condut**or** | Condut**ora** |
| Seller | Vended**or** | Vended**ora** |
| Sir | Senh**or** | Senh**ora** |

Nouns ending in "E":

| English | Masculine | Feminine |
|---------|-----------|----------|
| Governor | Governant**e** | Governant**a** |
| Master | Mestr**e** | Mestr**a** |
| Prince / Princess (that are not heirs to the throne) | Infant**e** | Infant**a** |

Adjectives ending in "OR," "ÊS," and "U"

| English | Masculine | Feminine |
|---------|-----------|----------|
| Charming | Encantad**or** | Encantad**ora** |
| Conservative | Conservad**or** | Conservad**ora** |
| French | Franc**ês** | Franc**esa** |
| English | Ingl**ês** | Ingl**esa** |

| Raw | Cr<u>u</u> | Cr<u>ua</u> |
| Naked | N<u>u</u> | N<u>ua</u> |

Nouns and adjectives ending in "EU":

| English | Masculine | Feminine |
|---|---|---|
| Commoner | Pleb<u>eu</u> | Pleb<u>eia</u> |
| European | Europ<u>eu</u> | Europ<u>eia</u> |
| Pigmee | Pigm<u>eu</u> | Pigm<u>eia</u> |

Nouns ending in "ÊS":

| English | Masculine | Feminine |
|---|---|---|
| Customer | Fregu<u>ês</u> | Fregues<u>a</u> |
| Marquis | Marqu<u>ês</u> | Marques<u>a</u> |
| Peasant | Campon<u>ês</u> | Campones<u>a</u> |

Exceptions to the rule:

| English | Masculine | Feminine |
|---|---|---|
| Husband / Wife | Marido | Mulher |
| Stepfather / Stepmother | Padrasto | Madrasta |
| Baron / Baroness | Barão | Baronesa |

| | | |
|---|---|---|
| Dog | Cão | Cadela |
| Actor / Actress | Actor | Actriz |
| Emperor / Empress | Imperador | Imperatriz |
| Jew | Judeu | Judia |
| Defendant | Réu | Ré |
| Hero / Heroin | Herói | Heroína |
| Poet | Poeta | Poetisa |
| Prince / Princess | Príncipe | Princesa |
| King / Queen | Rei | Rainha |

## Prepositions of place

Prepositions are a word class that functions as the connection of the meaning within a sentence, *i.e.,* two parts of a phrase are dependent on each other to make sense, and the preposition connects them.

| Preposições de lugar | |
|---|---|
| Above | Por cima |
| Around | Em volta de |
| At | Em |
| Behind of | Atrás de |

| | |
|---|---|
| Beside | Ao lado de |
| Between | Entre |
| Far from | Longe de |
| In front of | Na frente de |
| In the | No / na |
| Inside of | Dentro de |
| Near to / next to | Perto de |
| On | Em cima de |
| Outside of/out of | Fora de |
| Under | Debaixo de |

# Adverbs of quantity, place, mode, affirmation, negation, and doubt

An adverb functions as an information provider about the verb – it can modify or characterize an action – further explaining how the verbal action is occurring. It can also modify the adjective or another adverb.

| Advérbios de quantidade / intensidade | |
|---|---|
| A lot | Imenso / Imensa / Bastante |
| Almost | Quase |

| Least | Menos |
|---|---|
| Little | Pouco / Pouca |
| More / Further | Mais |
| Much / Very | Muito / Muita |
| Sufficiently | Suficientemente |
| Too | Demais |
| Too much | Demasiado |

## Advérbios de lugar

| | |
|---|---|
| Above | Acima |
| Below | Abaixo |
| Here | Aqui |
| Inside | Adentro |
| Nowhere | Nenhures |
| Over there, beyond | Além |
| Over there, in there | Ali |
| Somewhere | Algures |

| There, then | Aí |
|---|---|

## Advérbios de modo

| Badly | Mal |
|---|---|
| Carefully | Cuidadosamente |
| Easily | Facilmente |
| Quickly | Rapidamente |
| Slowly | Devagar |
| Slowly | Lentamente |
| Thus, therefore | Assim |
| Well, right | Bem |

## Advérbios de afirmação

| Certainly | Certamente |
|---|---|
| Effectively | Efectivamente |
| Really | Realmente |
| Surely | Decerto |

| Yes | Sim |
|-----|-----|

## Advérbios de negação

| Neither | Nem |
|---------|-----|
| Never | Nunca |
| Never ever | Jamais |
| No | Não |
| Nor, neither | Tampouco |

## Advérbios de dúvida

| Apparently | Aparentemente |
|------------|---------------|
| Maybe | Talvez |
| Perhaps | Quiçá |
| Possibly | Possivelmente |
| Probably | Provavelmente |
| Supposedly | Supostamente |

# Pronouns – subject, interrogative, direct & indirect object, possessive, indefinite, and relative

Pronouns exist to substitute or represent the nouns or names in a sentence.

| Subject pronouns | |
|---|---|
| I | Eu |
| You | Tu |
| He / She / It | Ele / Ela |
| Us | Nós |
| We | Vós |
| They | Eles / Elas |

| Interrogative pronouns | |
|---|---|
| What | Que |
| Who | Quem |
| Which | Qual |
| Which | Quais |
| How much | Quanto / Quanta |

| How many | Quantos /Quantas |
|---|---|

| Direct object pronouns | |
|---|---|
| Me | Me |
| You | Te |
| Him / Her / It | O / A |
| Us | Nos |
| You | Vos |
| Them | Os / As |

| Indirect object pronouns | |
|---|---|
| Me | Me |
| You | Te |
| Him / Her / It | Lhe |
| Us | Nos |
| You | Vos |
| Them | Lhes |

| Possessive pronouns | | |
|---|---|---|
| **English** | **Singular** | **Plural** |
| Mine | Meu / Minha | Meus / Minhas |
| Yours | Teu / Tua | Teus / Tuas |
| His / Hers | Seu / Sua | Seus / Suas |
| Ours | Nosso / Nossa | Nossos / Nossas |
| Yours | Vosso / Vossa | Vossos / Vossas |
| Theirs | Seu / Sua | Seus / Suas |

| Indefinite pronouns | |
|---|---|
| **Variable** | **invariable** |
| Algum, alguma, alguns, algumas (some / any / a few) | Alguém (someone / somebody) |
| Nenhum, nenhuma, nenhuns, nenhumas (none) | Ninguém (no one, nobody) |
| Todo, toda, todos, todas (all) | Tudo (everything) |
| Outro, outra, outros, outras (other) | Outrem (other) |

| | |
|---|---|
| Muito, muita, muitos, muitas (many) | Nada (nothing) |
| Pouco, pouca, poucos, poucas (few) | Quem (whoever) |
| Certo, certa, certos, certas (certain) | Cada (each / every) |
| Vários, várias (several) | Algo (something) |
| Tanto, tanta, tantos, tantas (as many) | |
| Quanto, quanta, quantos, quantas (how many) | |
| Qualquer, quaisquer (any / anything) | |

| Relative pronouns | |
|---|---|
| **Variable** | **Invariable** |
| O qual, a qual, os quais, as quais | Quem |
| Cujo, cuja, cujos, cujas | Que |
| Quanto, quanta, quantos, quantas | Onde |

# Comparatives and superlatives of adjectives

Adjectives are used to attribute traits or characteristics to nouns. The comparative degree is a construction that allows for a comparison of one or more traits between two or more people. The superlative degree establishes a more intense relationship between one entity amongst (many) other things.

| Normal / positive | Superiority comparative | Relative superlative of superiority | Synthetic absolute superlative |
|---|---|---|---|
| Bom (good) | Melhor (better) | O melhor (the best) | Óptimo (great) |
| Mau (bad) | Pior (worse) | O pior (the worst) | Péssimo (awful) |
| Grande (big) | Maior (bigger) | O maior (the biggest) | Enorme (enormous) |
| Pequeno (small) | Menor (smaller) | O menor (the smallest) | Mínimo (minimal) |
| Difícil (hard) | Mais difícil | O mais difícil | Dificílimo |
| Doce (sweet) | Mais doce | O mais doce | Dulcíssimo / docíssimo |
| Fácil (easy) | Mais fácil | O mais fácil | Facílimo |
| Feio (ugly) | Mais feio | O mais feio | Feiíssimo |

| | | | |
|---|---|---|---|
| Feliz (happy) | Mais feliz | O mais feliz | Felicíssimo |
| Horrível (horrible) | Mais horrível | O mais horrível | Horribilíssimo |
| Pobre (poor) | Mais pobre | O mais pobre | Paupérrimo |
| Rico (rich) | Mais rico | O mais rico | Riquíssimo |
| Simpático (nice) | Mais simpático | O mais simpático | Simpaticíssimo |
| Triste (triste) | Mais triste | O mais triste | Tristíssimo |

## Present tense of regular verbs

Regular verbs are the verbs that keep their stem constant throughout the whole process of conjugation – only the suffix changes.

With verbs ending in "**AR,**" after the stem, you just need to add – "**O,**" "**AS,**" "**A,**" "**AMOS,**" "**AIS,**" and "**AM.**" For instance:

| Verbo AMAR (to love) | |
|---|---|
| Eu | Am**o** |
| Tu | Am**as** |
| Ele/a | Am**a** |
| Nós | Am**amos** |
| Vós | Am**ais** |

| Eles/as | Am**am** |
|---------|----------|

With verbs ending in **"ER,"** after the stem, you just need to add – **"O," "ES," "E," "EMOS," "EIS,"** and **"EM."** For instance:

## Verbo VIVER (to live)

| Eu | Viv**o** |
|----|----------|
| Tu | Viv**es** |
| Ele/a | Viv**e** |
| Nós | Viv**emos** |
| Vós | Viv**éis** |
| Eles/as | Viv**em** |

With verbs ending in **"IR,"** after the stem, you just need to add – **"O," "ES," "E," "IMOS," "IS,"** and **"EM."** For instance:

## Verbo PARTIR (to break)

| Eu | Part**o** |
|----|-----------|
| Tu | Part**es** |
| Ele/a | Part**e** |
| Nós | Part**imos** |
| Vós | Part**is** |

| Eles/as | Part**em** |
|---------|------------|

## Present tense of irregular verbs

The only way to identify and conjugate irregular verbs is to study and memorize them – there is no other way around it.

## Future tense of regular & irregular verbs

To conjugate a verb in the future tense, you just need to add the endings **"EI," "ÁS," "Á," "EMOS," "EIS,"** and **"ÃO"** to the verb in its *infinitive form* (base form). For instance:

| Verbo DAR (to give) ||
|------------|------------|
| Eu | Darei |
| Tu | Darás |
| Ele/a | Dará |
| Nós | Daremos |
| Vós | Dareis |
| Eles/as | Darão |

| Verbo HAVER ||
|------------|------------|
| Eu | Haverei |
| Tu | Haverás |

| | |
|---|---|
| Ele/a | Haverá |
| Nós | Haveremos |
| Vós | Havereis |
| Eles/as | Haverão |

## Verbo PARTIR (to break)

| | |
|---|---|
| Eu | Partirei |
| Tu | Partirás |
| Ele/a | Partirá |
| Nós | Partiremos |
| Vós | Partireis |
| Eles/as | Partirão |

## Verbo IR

| | |
|---|---|
| Eu | Irei |
| Tu | Irás |
| Ele/a | Irá |

| | |
|---|---|
| Nós | Iremos |
| Vós | Ireis |
| Eles/as | Irão |

This rule applies to regular and irregular verbs and has only three exceptions:

## Verbo FAZER (to do)

| | |
|---|---|
| Eu | Farei |
| Tu | Farás |
| Ele/a | Fará |
| Nós | Faremos |
| Vós | Fareis |
| Eles/as | Farão |

## Verbo TRAZER (to bring)

| | |
|---|---|
| Eu | Trarei |
| Tu | Trarás |
| Ele/a | Trará |
| Nós | Traremos |

| | |
|---|---|
| Vós | Trareis |
| Eles/as | Trarão |

| Verbo DIZER (to say) | |
|---|---|
| Eu | Direi |
| Tu | Dirás |
| Ele/a | Dirá |
| Nós | Diremos |
| Vós | Direis |
| Eles/as | Dirão |

# Past tenses of regular verbs

## Simple past

The simple past is used to indicate an action that occurred in a determined moment of the past – it's a one-time action.

With verbs ending in **"AR"** after the stem, you just need to add – **"EI," "ASTE," "OU," "ÁMOS," "ASTES,"** and **"ARAM."** For instance:

| Verbo AMAR (to love) ||
| --- | --- |
| Eu | Amei |
| Tu | Amaste |
| Ele/a | Amou |
| Nós | Amámos |
| Vós | Amastes |
| Eles/as | Amaram |

With verbs ending in **"ER"** after the stem, you just need to add – **"I," "ESTE," "EU," "EMOS," "ESTES,"** and **"ERAM."** For instance:

| Verbo VIVER (to live) ||
| --- | --- |
| Eu | Vivi |
| Tu | Viveste |
| Ele/a | Viveu |
| Nós | Vivemos |
| Vós | Vivestes |
| Eles/as | Viveram |

With verbs ending in **"IR"** after the stem, you just need to add – **"I," "ISTE," "IU," "IMOS," "ISTES,"** and **"IRAM."** For instance:

| Verbo PARTIR (to break) ||
|---|---|
| Eu | Parti |
| Tu | Partiste |
| Ele/a | Partiu |
| Nós | Partimos |
| Vós | Partistes |
| Eles/as | Partiram |

### Past continuous

The past continuous is used to indicate an action that wasn't concluded, to indicate something that happened in the past that was ongoing.

With verbs ending in **"AR"** after the stem, you just need to add – **"AVA," "AVAS," "AVA," "ÁVAMOS," "ÁVEIS,"** and **"AVAM."** For instance:

| Verbo AMAR (to love) ||
|---|---|
| Eu | Amava |
| Tu | Amavas |
| Ele/a | Amava |
| Nós | Amávamos |

| | |
|---|---|
| Vós | Amáveis |
| Eles/as | Amavam |

With verbs ending in **"ER" and "IR"** after the stem, you just need to add – **"IA," "IAS," "IA," "IAMOS," "ÍEIS,"** and **"IAM."** For instance:

| Verbo VIVER (to live) ||
|---|---|
| Eu | Vivia |
| Tu | Vivias |
| Ele/a | Vivia |
| Nós | Vivíamos |
| Vós | Vivíeis |
| Eles/as | Viviam |

| Verbo PARTIR (to break) ||
|---|---|
| Eu | Partia |
| Tu | Partias |
| Ele/a | Partia |
| Nós | Partíamos |

| Vós | Partíeis |
|---|---|
| Eles/as | Partiam |

### Past tenses of irregular verbs

The only way to identify and conjugate irregular verbs is to study and memorize them – there is no other way around it.

# Vocabulary Appendix

In this chapter you will find a compilation of the vocabulary learned in the previous chapters. There is just a little twist: this will be a homemade dictionary. What this means is that instead of it being complete with the English words and correspondent Portuguese translations, this glossary will only have the English words, leaving it up to you to fill in the correct translation in Portuguese.

Where applicable, you will also have to write the feminine form of the word. Do not worry about making mistakes – you can always go back to the chapter where you were supposed to learn these words to check out the correct spelling. The first words in each table will be filled out for you to get going!

Just a little tip for you to be able to memorize all the vocabulary provided in around a month: you can, in one day, study one chapter, read it carefully, and diligently take notes. Take another day to practice memorizing the words you learned through flashcards. Finally, take the third day to try to fill in the blanks in this dictionary.

# PORTUGUESE BASICS - Colors

| | |
|---|---|
| Beige | |
| Black | |
| Blue | |
| Brown | |
| Burgundy | |
| Gold | |
| Gray | |
| Green | |
| Orange | |
| Pink | |
| Purple | |
| Red | |
| Silver | |
| Turquoise | |
| White | |
| Yellow | |

# PORTUGUESE BASICS - Numbers

| | |
|---|---|
| Zero | |
| One | |
| Two | |
| Three | |
| Four | |
| Five | |
| Six | |
| Seven | |
| Eight | |
| Nine | |
| Ten | |
| Eleven | |
| Twelve | |
| Thirteen | |
| Fourteen | |
| Fifteen | |

| | |
|---|---|
| Sixteen | |
| Seventeen | |
| Eighteen | |
| Nineteen | |
| Twenty | |

## MEETING NEW PEOPLE - Countries

| Country | Country in Portuguese | Nationality in Portuguese |
|---|---|---|
| Afghanistan | | |
| Argentina | | |
| Australia | | |
| Belarus | | |
| Belgium | | |
| Brazil | | |
| Canada | | |
| Cape Verde | | |

| | | |
|---|---|---|
| China | | |
| Colombia | | |
| Croatia | | |
| Denmark | | |
| East Timor | | |
| Ecuador | | |
| Egypt | | |
| England | | |
| France | | |
| Germany | | |
| Greece | | |
| Guinea-Bissau | | |
| India | | |
| Iran | | |
| Iraq | | |
| Ireland | | |
| Italy | | |

| | | |
|---|---|---|
| Japan | | |
| Mexico | | |
| Morocco | | |
| Mozambique | | |
| Netherlands | | |
| New Zealand | | |
| Nigeria | | |
| North Korea | | |
| Paraguay | | |
| Russia | | |
| São Tomé and Príncipe | | |
| Saudi Arabia | | |
| Scotland | | |
| Serbia | | |
| South Africa | | |
| South Korea | | |
| Spain | | |

| | | |
|---|---|---|
| Sweden | | |
| Switzerland | | |
| Turkey | | |
| Ukraine | | |
| United States of America | | |
| Uruguay | | |
| Venezuela | | |

## MEETING NEW PEOPLE – Numbers over 20

| English | Portuguese |
|---|---|
| Twenty | |
| Thirty | |
| Forty | |
| Fifty | |
| Sixty | |
| Seventy | |

| English | Portuguese |
|---------|------------|
| Eighty | |
| Ninety | |
| One hundred | |

## CHECKING INTO YOUR ROOM – Parts & rooms of the house

| English | Portuguese |
|---------|------------|
| Apartment | |
| Attic | |
| Backyard | |
| Balcony | |
| Basement | |
| Bathroom | |
| Bathtub | |
| Chimney | |
| Closet | |
| Corridor | |

| | |
|---|---|
| Dining room | |
| Door | |
| Garage | |
| Garden | |
| Guest room | |
| Hall | |
| House | |
| Kid's room | |
| Kitchen | |
| Kitchen sink | |
| Laundry room | |
| Library | |
| Living room | |
| Nursery | |
| Office | |
| Pantry | |
| Roof | |

| English | Portuguese |
|---------|------------|
| Room, bedroom | |
| Sink | |
| Stairs | |
| Toilet | |
| Utility/storeroom | |
| Window | |
| Wine cellar | |

## CHECKING INTO YOUR ROOM – Objects of the house

| English | Portuguese |
|---------|------------|
| Backpack | |
| Bag | |
| Bed | |
| Book | |
| Bottle | |
| Bowl | |

| | |
|---|---|
| Candle | |
| Clock | |
| Cradle/crib | |
| Cup | |
| Cutlery | |
| Dishes | |
| Door lock | |
| Flashlight | |
| Fork | |
| Furniture | |
| Glass (of water) | |
| Glass (of a window) | |
| Knife | |
| Lighter | |
| Magazines | |
| Matches | |
| Mirror | |

| | |
|---|---|
| Napkin | |
| Newspaper | |
| Pen | |
| Pencil | |
| Plate | |
| Pot | |
| Scissors | |
| Sleeping bag | |
| Sofa | |
| Spoon | |
| Tablecloth | |
| Telephone | |
| Television | |
| Toilet paper | |
| Toothbrush | |
| Toothpaste | |
| Umbrella | |

| Utensils | |
|----------|---|

## GOING SHOPPING – Fruits & vegetables

| English | Portuguese |
|---------|------------|
| Apple | |
| Avocado | |
| Banana | |
| Blackberry | |
| Blueberry | |
| Broccoli | |
| Cabbage | |
| Carrot | |
| Cherry | |
| Coconut | |
| Cranberry | |
| Eggplant | |
| Garlic | |

| | |
|---|---|
| Gooseberry | |
| Grapes | |
| Leek | |
| Lemon | |
| Lettuce | |
| Lime | |
| Mango | |
| Mushroom | |
| Nuts | |
| Onion | |
| Orange | |
| Papaya | |
| Peaches | |
| Pear | |
| Pineapple | |
| Potato | |
| Raspberry | |

| | |
|---|---|
| Strawberries | |
| Sweet Potato | |
| Tomato | |
| Vegetables | |
| Zucchini | |

| GOING SHOPPING – At the supermarket ||
|---|---|
| **English** | **Portuguese** |
| Barley | |
| Beef | |
| Beer | |
| Bread | |
| Butter | |
| Cereal | |
| Cheese | |
| Chocolate | |
| Coffee | |

| | |
|---|---|
| Corn | |
| Crackers | |
| Egg | |
| Fish | |
| Flesh | |
| Flour | |
| Ham | |
| Ice cream | |
| Jam | |
| Juice | |
| Meat | |
| Milk | |
| Oat | |
| Olive Oil | |
| Olives | |
| Peanut Butter | |
| Peanuts | |

| English | Portuguese |
|---------|------------|
| Pepper | |
| Salt | |
| Sandwich | |
| Sausage | |
| Sugar | |
| Tea | |
| Vinegar | |
| Water | |
| Wine | |

## GOING SIGHTSEEING – Transportation

| English | Portuguese |
|---------|------------|
| Airplane | |
| Bicycle | |
| Boat | |
| Bus | |
| Canoe | |

| | |
|---|---|
| Car | |
| Cruise ship | |
| Ferry | |
| Helicopter | |
| Motorbike | |
| Scooter | |
| Ship | |
| Taxi | |
| Trailer | |
| Train | |
| Tram | |
| Truck | |
| Underground | |
| Van | |

## GOING SIGHTSEEING – Giving directions

| English | Portuguese |
|---|---|
| Close | |
| Crossroads | |
| Far | |
| Go down this street | |
| Go over | |
| Go under | |
| Go up this street | |
| Left | |
| Right | |
| Roundabout | |
| Straight ahead | |
| To continue | |
| To cross | |
| To follow | |
| To go until | |

| | |
|---|---|
| To turn | |
| On the other side | |

| GOING SIGHTSEEING – Buildings in twon | |
|---|---|
| **English** | **Portuguese** |
| Airport | |
| Bakery | |
| Bank | |
| Book Shop | |
| Bus station | |
| Bus stop | |
| Butcher's | |
| Café | |
| Church | |
| Clothes shop | |
| Dentist | |
| Fire Station | |

| | |
|---|---|
| Gyn | |
| Hairdresser's | |
| Hospital | |
| Museum | |
| Police Station | |
| Posto Office | |
| Restaurant | |
| School | |
| Shop | |
| Supermarket | |
| Theater | |
| Train station | |
| Zoo | |

## GOING SIGHTSEEING – Time expressions for the present

| English | Portuguese |
|---|---|
| In a little while | |
| In a minute | |
| In an hour | |
| In this moment | |
| Later | |
| Now | |
| Right now | |
| Soon | |
| The time has come | |
| Today | |
| Tomorrow | |

# HAVING A HOUSE PARTY – Family members

| English | Portuguese |
|---|---|
| Aunt | |
| Best friend | |
| Boyfriend | |
| Brother | |
| Brother-in-law | |
| Cousin | |
| Daughter | |
| Daughter-in-law | |
| Family | |
| Father-in-law | |
| Fiancé | |
| Friend | |
| Girlfriend | |
| Goddaughter | |
| Godfather | |

| | |
|---|---|
| Godmother | |
| Godson | |
| Granddaughter | |
| Grandfather | |
| Grandmother | |
| Grandparents | |
| Grandson | |
| Husband | |
| Mother-in-law | |
| Nephew | |
| Niece | |
| Sister | |
| Sister-in-law | |
| Son | |
| Son-in-law | |
| Stepdaughter | |
| Stepfather | |

| | |
|---|---|
| Stepmother | |
| Stepson | |
| Uncle | |
| Wife | |

## HAVING A HOUSE PARTY – The human body

| English | Portuguese |
|---|---|
| Aunt | |
| Best friend | |
| Boyfriend | |
| Brother | |
| Brother-in-law | |
| Cousin | |
| Daughter | |
| Daughter-in-law | |
| Family | |
| Father-in-law | |

| | |
|---|---|
| Fiancé | |
| Friend | |
| Girlfriend | |
| Goddaughter | |
| Godfather | |
| Godmother | |
| Godson | |
| Granddaughter | |
| Grandfather | |
| Grandmother | |
| Grandparents | |
| Grandson | |
| Husband | |
| Mother-in-law | |
| Nephew | |
| Niece | |
| Sister | |

| | |
|---|---|
| Sister-in-law | |
| Son | |
| Son-in-law | |
| Stepdaughter | |
| Stepfather | |
| Stepmother | |
| Stepson | |
| Uncle | |
| Wife | |

## HAVING A HOUSE PARTY – Describing people's appearance

| English | Portuguese |
|---|---|
| Bald ≠ Hairy | |
| Beautiful ≠ Ugly | |
| Dark ≠ light skin | |
| Gorgeous ≠ Hideous | |

| | |
|---|---|
| Muscular ≠ Slim | |
| Short ≠ long hair | |
| Tall ≠ Short | |
| Tanned ≠ Pale | |
| Thin ≠ Fat | |
| Young ≠ Old | |

## EATING OUT – Meals

| English | Portuguese |
|---|---|
| Breakfast | |
| Lunch | |
| Supper | |
| Dinner | |
| Meal | |
| Food | |
| Drink | |
| Snack | |

# EATING OUT – Expressing likes & dislikes

| English | Portuguese |
|---|---|
| I like... | |
| I love... | |
| I adore... | |
| I'm crazy about... | |
| I'm mad about... | |
| I enjoy... | |
| I have a soft spot for... | |
| I'm interested in... | |
| I'm in love with... | |
| I have a crush on... | |
| I hate... | |
| I can't bear... | |
| I detest... | |

| EATING OUT – Interjections | |
| --- | --- |
| **English** | **Portuguese** |
| Ai! | |
| Enough! | |
| Dang! | |
| Good! | |
| Let's go! | |
| Yes sir! | |
| Let's go! | |
| Congratulations! | |
| Go for it! | |
| Gee! | |
| My God! | |
| Heavens! | |
| Jesus! | |
| Thank God! | |
| I wish! | |

| | |
|---|---|
| If God wills! | |
| I wish! | |
| I'll be a monkey's uncle! | |
| Nice! | |

## AT THE MOVIES – Telling the time & date

| English | Portuguese |
|---|---|
| Monday | |
| Tuesday | |
| Wednesday | |
| Thursday | |
| Friday | |
| Saturday | |
| Sunday | |

| AT THE MOVIES – Ordinal numerals | |
|---|---|
| **English** | **Portuguese** |
| First | |
| Second | |
| Third | |
| Forth | |
| Fifth | |
| Sixth | |
| Seventh | |
| Eight | |
| Ninth | |
| Tenth | |
| Twentieth | |
| Thirtieth | |
| Fortieth | |
| Fiftieth | |
| Sixtieth | |

| | |
|---|---|
| Seventieth | |
| Eightieth | |
| Ninetieth | |
| Hundreth | |

## AT THE MOVIES – Describing people's personality

| English | Portuguese |
|---|---|
| Adventurous | |
| Ambitious | |
| Anxious | |
| Bad-tempered | |
| Bossy | |
| Calm | |
| Careful | |
| Careless | |
| Cheerful | |
| Confident | |

| | |
|---|---|
| Courageous | |
| Crazy | |
| Creative | |
| Determined | |
| Discreet | |
| Dishonest | |
| Distracted | |
| Emotional | |
| Energetic | |
| Faithful | |
| Fearless | |
| Friendly | |
| Funny | |
| Generous | |
| Gentle | |
| Happy | |
| Hard-working | |

| | |
|---|---|
| Helpful | |
| Honest | |
| Humble | |
| Hypocritical | |
| Impatient | |
| Intelligent | |
| Jealous | |
| Kind | |
| Lazy | |
| Loyal | |
| Mean | |
| Modest | |
| Nervous | |
| Nice | |
| Optimistic | |
| Patient | |
| Persistent | |

| | |
|---|---|
| Pessimistic | |
| Polite | |
| Popular | |
| Proud | |
| Rational | |
| Reliable | |
| Romantic | |
| Rude | |
| Selfish | |
| Sensible | |
| Sensitive | |
| Serious | |
| Shy | |
| Sincere | |
| Smart | |
| Sociable | |
| Stubborn | |

| | |
|---|---|
| Talkative | |
| Worried | |

## TALKING ABOUT THE PAST – Time expressions for past events

| English | Portuguese |
|---|---|
| A few days ago | |
| Last Sunday | |
| Last week | |
| Last year | |
| Some time ago | |
| The day before yesterday | |
| Yesterday | |
| Yesterday night | |

# TALKING ABOUT THE PAST – Months & Seasons

| English | Portuguese |
|---|---|
| Months | |
| January | |
| February | |
| March | |
| April | |
| May | |
| June | |
| July | |
| August | |
| September | |
| October | |
| November | |
| December | |
| Spring | |
| Summer | |

| | |
|---|---|
| Autumn/Fall | |
| Winter | |
| Easter | |
| Christmas | |
| Christmas Eve | |
| New Year | |
| New Year's Eve | |
| April Fool's Day | |
| Halloween | |

## TALKING ABOUT THE PAST – Jobs & Professions

| English | Portuguese |
|---|---|
| Accountant | |
| Actress | |
| Archaeologist | |
| Architect | |
| Ballet dancer | |

| | |
|---|---|
| Bank clerk | |
| Biologist | |
| Chemist | |
| Doctor | |
| Engineer | |
| Firefighter | |
| Hairstylist | |
| Judge | |
| Lawyer | |
| Mechanic | |
| Nurse | |
| Painter | |
| Poet | |
| Psychologist | |
| Saleswoman | |
| Singer | |
| Student | |

| | |
|---|---|
| Surgeon | |
| Teacher | |
| Veterinarian | |
| Writer | |

# Answer Key

In this chapter, you can find the answers - not to all of your problems - but at least to the questions you were trying to solve during the course of this book. For the quizzes in chapter 5 and chapter 9, you will be able to attribute a score to your own performance and check if you passed or not. If you didn't, you should go back to the lessons in which you struggled the most and read them again. Not to worry, though - this isn't an exam, and you shouldn't feel discouraged if you don't pass it the first time around. The score is only a way for you to be certain that the information that was taught was definitely retained and absorbed so that you can move on to the next quiz, sure of what you learned in the previous chapters.

## Chapter 2

1) Underline the subject pronouns and different forms of the verb "to be" in the dialogue found in the beginning of the chapter.

- *Bom dia!* ***Eu sou*** *o John. Como te chamas?*

- *Olá, John.* ***Eu sou*** *o Tom. Como* ***estás****?*

- *Bem, obrigado. E* ***tu****?*

- *Está tudo bem, obrigado. Que idade tens?*

- *Tenho 31 anos. De onde és?*

- *Eu sou de Lisboa. E tu? Qual é a tua nacionalidade?*

- *Eu sou um americano de Nova Iorque.*

2) **Rewrite all of the nationalities but this time in the feminine form.**

| Masculine | Feminine | Masculine | Feminine |
|---|---|---|---|
| **Afegão** | Afegã | **Iraquiano** | Iraquiana |
| **Alemão** | Alemã | **Irlandês** | Irlandesa |
| **Americano** | Americana | **Italiano** | Italiana |
| **Argentino** | Argentina | **Japonês** | Japonesa |
| **Australiano** | Australiana | **Marroquino** | Marroquina |
| **Belga** | Belga | **Mexicano** | Mexicana |
| **Bielorrusso** | Bielorrussa | **Moçambicano** | Moçambicana |
| **Brasileiro** | Brasileira | **Neozelandês** | Neozelandesa |
| **Cabo-verdiano** | Cabo-verdiana | **Neozelandês** | Neozelandesa |
| **Canadiano** | Canadiana | **Nigeriano** | Nigeriana |

| | | | |
|---|---|---|---|
| Chinês | Chinesa | Norte-coreano | Norte-coeana |
| Colombiano | Colombiana | Paraguaio | Paraguaia |
| Croata | Croata | Russo | Russa |
| Dinamarquês | Dinamarquesa | São-tomense | São-tomense |
| Egípcio | Egípcia | Saudita | Saudita |
| Equatoriano | Equatoriana | Sérvio | Sérvia |
| Escocês | Escocesa | Sueco | Sueca |
| Espanhol | Espanhola | Suíço | Suíça |
| Francês | Francesa | Sul-africano | Sul-africana |
| Grego | Grega | Sul-coreano | Sul-coreana |
| Guineense | Guineense | Timorense | Timorense |
| Holandês | Holandesa | Turco | Turca |
| Indiano | Indiana | Ucraniano | Ucraniana |
| Inglês | Inglesa | Uruguaio | Urugaia |
| Iraniano | Iraniana | Venezuelano | Venezuelana |

# Chapter 3

1) Complete the following sentences with the correct definite or indefinite articles.

<u>O</u> gato é preto. (The cat is black.)

Só <u>os</u> santos vão para o céu. (Only saints go to heaven.)

Esta é <u>a</u> namorada do meu irmão. (This is my brother's girlfriend.)

<u>As</u> ruas estão vazias. (The streets are empty.)

2) Complete the following sentences with the correct indefinite articles.

Estão **umas** uvas na mesa. (There are some grapes on the table.)

Eu quero **uma** maçã. (I want an apple.)

**Um** americano falou comigo. (An American talked to me.)

Ele quer **uns** calções azuis. (He wants blue shorts.)

3) Complete the following sentences using the correct prepositions of place.

A minha escola é **longe de** casa. (My school is far away from home.)

A bola está **em cima** da caixa. (The ball is on the box.)

Eu vivo **perto da** praia. (I live near the beach.)

Os talheres estão **na** despensa. (The cuttlery are in the pantry.)

Ele vive **debaixo** da ponte. (He lives under the bridge.)

O relógio está **por cima** do sofá. (The clock is above the sofa.)

Está uma pessoa **dentro de** casa. (There is a person inside the house.)

# Chapter 5 – Quiz

1) Turn the following sentences into questions, affirmative or negative statements.

Eu gosto de chocolate. – **Eu não gosto de chocolate.**

Ele foi à escola. – **Ele foi à escola?**

Nós não queremos ir ao hospital. – **Nós queremos ir à escola.**

Eles não são Portugueses? **Eles são Portugueses.**

Tu pescas todos os dias? – **Tu não pescas todos os dias?**

2) **Mark the words that are correctly following the rules of capitalization.**

| | | |
|---|---|---|
| – rio Tejo | – Rua Augusta | – usa |
| – segunda guerra mundial | – (homem) espanhol | – outono |
| – quarta-feira | – janeiro | – Natal |
| – Dezembro | – Domingo | – John |

3) **Complete the blank spaces with the correct form of the verb** *to be* **(either "SER" or "ESTAR").**

Eu **sou** careca.

**Está** frio hoje.

Tu **és** alto.

Nós **estamos** cansadas.

Eles **são/estão**[42] casados?

Ela **está** ali.

O meu cão **é** castanho.

4) **Allocate the words below to their correct place on the table.**

| Adverbs of place | Adverbs of quantity | Prepositions of place |
|---|---|---|
| Algures | Demais | Entre |
| Abaixo | Imenso | Longe |

---

42 This was actually a tricky one. Being married is, as you know, not an unchangeable state of things, but it tends to be, or at least that's how it was in the past, more or less constant. Hence, in Portuguese, people normally use the verb "SER" than the verb "ESTAR." You can, however, use any of these verbs when referring to the marital status of somebody.

---

5) Conjugate the following verbs in the present tense: "ESTUDAR," "COMER," "CUMPRIR," and "FAZER."

| Verbo ESTUDAR (to study) | |
| --- | --- |
| Eu | Estudo |
| Tu | Estudas |
| Ele/a | Estuda |
| Nós | Estudamos |
| Vós | Estudais |
| Eles/as | Estudam |

| Verbo COMER (to eat) | |
| --- | --- |
| Eu | Como |
| Tu | Comes |
| Ele/a | Come |
| Nós | Comemos |
| Vós | Comeis |
| Eles/as | Comem |

| Verbo CUMPRIR (to comply/fulfill) ||
|---|---|
| Eu | Cumpro |
| Tu | Cumpres |
| Ele/a | Cumpre |
| Nós | Cumprimos |
| Vós | Cumpris |
| Eles/as | Cumprem |

| Verbo FAZER (to do) ||
|---|---|
| Eu | Faço |
| Tu | Fazes |
| Ele/a | Faz |
| Nós | Fazemos |
| Vós | Fazeis |
| Eles/as | Fazem |

6) Identify the mood – indicative, subjunctive, or imperative – in which the following verbs are conjugated. (The tense in which the verbs are conjugated will also be identified even though it wasn't required in the question.)

Come imediatamente! – Imperative mood (affirmative)

A minha professora quer que eu estude mais. – Subjunctive mood (present tense)

Ele não dorme bem. – Indicative mood (presente tense)

Vós sereis os melhores. – Indicative mood (future tense)

Tu farias isso por mim? – Indicative mood (conditional)

Eu gostava que tu sorrisses mais. – Subjunctive mood (imperfect tense)

Não corras por favor! – Imperative mood (negative)

# Chapter 8

The parts of the sheet about the personality and appearance traits of the main character are obviously mere suggestions since there are synonyms of the traits written down –

or other characteristics you could use to describe him.

---

## CHARACTER SHEET

Name: **João Fernandes**

Age: **around 40**

Gender: **Male**

Occupation: **Landowner**

Marital status: **Married**

Appearance:

- **Brown hair**
- **Tall**
- **Lean**

Personality:

- **Arrogant**
- **Overbearing**
- **Powerful**

---

# Chapter 9 - Quiz

1) Identify only the direct object in the following sentences and substitute it for the correct pronoun.

 - Eu emprestei-*a*. (I lent it.)

 - A Rita e a Leonor fazem-*nos*. (Rita and Leonor do it.)

 - Eu não *o* quero. (I don't want it.)

 - Ele vai dá-*lo* à namorada. (He will give it to the girlfriend.)

 - Quem *o* contou? (Who told it?)

 - A Rita e a Leonor também *os* fazem. (Rita and Leonor also do them.)

2) Identify only the indirect object in the following sentences and substitute it for the correct pronoun.

 - A Teresa estragou-*lhe* a cama. (Teresa ruined her bed.)

 - O cão sujou-*lhe* o chão. (The dog stained his floor.)

 - Ele vai dar-*lhe* um presente. (He will give her a present.)

 - O meu pai queria abraçar-*te*. (My father wanted to hug you.)

 - Os ladrões queriam fazer-*nos* mal. (The thieves wanted to hurt us.)

 - Elas fizeram-*lhes* as malas. (They packed their suitcases.)

3) Now substitute the direct and indirect object for the correct pronouns.

 - Ele vai dar-*lho*. (He will give it to her.)

 - A Teresa estragou-*lha*. (Teresa ruined her sister's bed.)

 - A Rita e a Leonor também *lhos* fazem. (Rita and Leonor also do them.)

 - O presidente ofereceu-*to*. (The president offered it to you.)

4) Fill out the blank spaces in the following table with the adjective adapted to the correspondent gender.

| English | Masculine | Feminine |
|---|---|---|
| Arrogant | Arrogante | **ARROGANTE** |
| Bald | **CARECA** | Careca |
| Bossy | Mandão | **MANDONA** |
| Champion | Campeão | **CAMPEÃ** |
| Charming | **ENCANTADOR** | Encantadora |
| Commoner | **PLEBEU** | Plebeia |
| Confident | Confiante | **CONFIANTE** |
| Conservative | Conservador | **CONSERVADOR** |
| Courteous | Cortês | **CORTÊS** |
| English | **INGLÊS** | Inglesa |
| European | Europeu | **EUROPEIA** |
| Faithful | Fiel | **FIEL** |
| Generous | Generoso | **GENEROSA** |
| Gentle | **GENTIL** | Gentil |

| | | |
|---|---|---|
| Healthy | São | **SÃ** |
| Hideous | Horrendo | **HORRENDA** |
| Idiot | **IDIOTA** | Idiota |
| Intelligent | Inteligente | **INTELIGENTE** |
| Muscular | Musculado | **MUSCULADA** |
| Naked | **NU** | Nua |
| Orphan | **ORFÃO** | Orfã |
| Raw | Cru | **CRUA** |
| Romantic | **ROMÂNTICO** | Romântica |
| Rude | Rude | **RUDE** |
| Sociable | Sociável | **SOCIÁVEL** |
| Stubborn | Teimoso | **TEIMOSA** |
| Talkative | Falador | **FALADORA** |
| Tanned | **BRONZEADO** | Bronzeada |

5) Underline the possessive adjectives in the sentences below and fill the blank spaces with the correct possessive pronouns.

- O **meu** cão não tem coleira. Este tem, logo deve ser o **TEU / SEU / VOSSO**. (My dog doesn't have a leash. This one has, so it must be yours.)

- A **tua** casa é enorme! A **MINHA** é tão pequena... (Your house is enormous! Mine is so small...)

- O professor disse que esta são as **vossas** guitarras. É verdade que são **VOSSAS**? (The professor said that these are your guitars. Is it true that they are yours?)

- Se eu tenho um problema, o problema não é **teu**, é **MEU**. (If I have a problem, it's not your problem, it's mine.)

6) Conjugate the following verbs in the <u>future tense of the indicative mood.</u>

| Verbo IR | |
|---|---|
| Eu | Irei |
| Tu | Irás |
| Ele / a | Irá |
| Nós | Iremos |
| Vós | Ireis |
| Eles / as | Irão |

| Verbo FICAR | |
|---|---|
| Eu | Ficarei |
| Tu | Ficarás |
| Ele / a | Ficará |
| Nós | Ficaremos |

| | |
|---|---|
| Vós | Ficareis |
| Eles / as | Ficarão |

| Verbo ESTAR | |
|---|---|
| Eu | Estarei |
| Tu | Estarás |
| Ele / a | Estará |
| Nós | Estaremos |
| Vós | Estareis |
| Eles / as | Estarão |

7) Underline the verbs conjugated in the past tense in the dialogue found in the beginning of chapter 9.

"Que bom estar de volta! **Tinha** muitas saudades vossas!

"Nós também **sentimos** a tua falta. Como **foram** as férias? Onde **estiveste**? Onde **foste**?

"**Foram** incríveis! **Conheci** pessoas novas, **passeei** muito por Lisboa... Enfim, tenho tanto para contar!

"Então, na viagem de avião **li** um panfleto que me **introduziu** à língua portuguesa; no avião **conheci** ainda um rapaz muito prestável chamado João que me **ensinou** umas coisas. Depois de fazer check-in no hotel, **fui** comprar estes presentes para vocês – gostam?

"Nos dias seguintes **andei** por Lisboa a conhecer a cidade e os monumentos históricos. E, claro, sempre a estudar e a absorver Português. Foi num desses dias que **conheci** uma guia – a Marta – que agora é minha amiga, e que me **convidou** para jantar na casa dela.

"Não, **estava** lá a família e amigos dela. E **eram** todos muitos simpáticos. **Visitei** ainda restaurantes típicos onde **comi** comida regional, e até **sobrou** tempo para ir ao cinema!

"Então **foram** umas férias para repetir?

8) Conjugate the following verbs in the <u>simple past tense of the indicative mood.</u>

| Verbo ANDAR (to walk) | |
|---|---|
| Eu | Andei |
| Tu | Andaste |
| Ele / a | Andou |

| | |
|---|---|
| Nós | Andámos |
| Vós | Andastes |
| Eles / as | Andaram |

## Verbo COMER (to eat)

| | |
|---|---|
| Eu | Comi |
| Tu | Comeste |
| Ele / a | Comeu |
| Nós | Comemos |
| Vós | Comestes |
| Eles / as | Comeram |

## Verbo SENTIR (to feel)

| | |
|---|---|
| Eu | Senti |
| Tu | Sentiste |
| Ele / a | Sentiu |
| Nós | Sentimos |

| Vós | Sentistes |
|---|---|
| Eles / as | Sentiram |

9) Conjugate the following verbs in the <u>past continuous of the indicative mood.</u>

| Verbo OLHAR (to look) | |
|---|---|
| Eu | Olhava |
| Tu | Olhavas |
| Ele/a | Olhava |
| Nós | Olhávamos |
| Vós | Olháveis |
| Eles/as | Olhavam |

| Verbo SABER (to know) | |
|---|---|
| Eu | Sabia |
| Tu | Sabias |
| Ele/a | Sabia |
| Nós | Sabíamos |
| Vós | Sabíeis |
| Eles/as | Sabiam |

| Verbo SORRIR (to smile) | |
| --- | --- |
| Eu | Sorria |
| Tu | Sorrias |
| Ele/a | Sorria |
| Nós | Sorríamos |
| Vós | Sorríeis |
| Eles/as | Sorriam |

# IPA Chart

IPA stands for International Phonemic Alphabet, which is an alphabetic system of phonetic notation that serves as an internationally standardized written representation of speech sounds. In the accompanying chart, you can find all the sounds that exist in the Portuguese language. Below each phonetic notation, which is called a grapheme, there is an example word that uses the sound in question.

Just so it is easier for you to grasp how the words and letters should be enunciated, there is also a table in which you can find English words that use equal or similar sounds to the ones represented by the graphemes. Bear in mind that these aren't, in some cases, totally accurate, but only approximations of what the grapheme should sound like.

## Vowels

| a<br>falámos | ɐ<br>falamos | ɐ̃<br>canto | e<br>crê | ẽ<br>dentro | ɛ<br>pé | i<br>vi | ɨ<br>se |
|---|---|---|---|---|---|---|---|
| ĩ<br>vim | ɔ<br>nós | o<br>pôs | õ<br>som | u<br>tu | ũ<br>mundo | j<br>saia | w<br>mau |

# Consonants

| b<br>bar | ð<br>cedo | d<br>dar | f<br>fazer | g<br>golo | ɣ<br>fogo | k<br>cor | l<br>lar |
|---|---|---|---|---|---|---|---|
| ɫ<br>sal | ʎ<br>galho | m<br>mato | n<br>nato | ɲ<br>pinha | p<br>pato | ʁ<br>rato | ɾ<br>cara |
| s<br>saco | ʃ<br>chato | tʃ<br>tchau | t<br>tacto | v<br>vale | z<br>zebra | | |

# English approximations

| a<br>father | ɐ<br>pub | ɐ̃<br>can't | e<br>they | ẽ<br>send | ɛ<br>set | i<br>see | ɨ<br>emission |
|---|---|---|---|---|---|---|---|
| ĩ<br>sing | ɔ<br>on | o<br>row | õ<br>long | u<br>foot | ũ<br>wound | j<br>you | w<br>quick |
| b<br>about | ð<br>the | d<br>today | f<br>fat | g<br>game | ɣ<br>between ago and hold | k<br>scam | l<br>lavender |

| ɫ | ʎ | m | n | ɲ | p | ʁ | ɾ |
|---|---|---|---|---|---|---|---|
| toll | ★ 43 | mole | not | ★ 44 | pull | rouge 45 | water 46 |

| s | ʃ | tʃ | t | v | z |
|---|---|---|---|---|---|
| sad | shoe | chees e | tall | vast | zebra |

---

43 The sound "LH" is not present in the English language, nor there is a word that is similar enough to convey the proper sound. Here is a Youtube video that may help you with the correct diction:
https://www.youtube.com/watch?v=ZHu9E8Y0_wI&ab_channel=TheSoundsofPortuguese

44 Just like the pair "LH," the sound "NH" is not present in the English language, nor there is a word that is similar enough to convey the proper sound. Check the following video to help you with the pronunciation of this sound:
https://www.youtube.com/watch?v=eV1pcZ9K0GY&ab_channel=TheSoundsofPortuguese

45 This is called a guttural "R," also present in the French language. It is a sound that comes from the throat, very similar to a human imitating a lion growling! Or in an alternate phonetic notation: "GRRRRR!"

46 The pronunciation of "WATER" in this case has to follow the general American-English accent, which rolls the "T" a little bit instead of enunciating a hard "T" like the general British-English accent would.